Praise for *Why Digital Transformations Fail*

"If you've ever wondered why digital disruption continues largely unabated, despite efforts of the world's top leaders, you're not alone. If you want a practical and clear-eyed playbook to help you do something about it, this book is for you."
—**Dr. Simone Ahuja, founder, Blood Orange, and author of *Disrupt-It-Yourself***

"This is the book I wish I had two decades ago. I would recommend Tony's book for anyone interested in digital transformation."
—**Josué Alencar, Springs Global, Brazil**

"A step-by-step guide for organizational leaders aiming to survive, thrive, and stay relevant in the age of digital disruption."
—**Oğuzhan Aygören, Assistant Professor of Marketing, Entrepreneurship, and Innovation, Boğaziçi University, Turkey**

"Tony has a fantastic track record for executing digital transformations successfully. His road map for making digital transformations successful is brilliant. Read this book and transform your business successfully!"
—**Caroline Basyn, Chief Information Officer and GBS Officer, Mondelēz International**

"Many executives will read this book after their digital strategy flops. Just as many will read it before they craft a winning plan. I suggest the latter."
—**Frank Casale, founder, Institute for Robotic Process Automation & Artificial Intelligence**

"This book should be read and reread by every leader in the private and public sectors. It's a primer on how to survive and win in the current digital industrial revolution."
—**Vivek Choudhury, Associate Dean for Strategic Initiatives and Professor of Information Systems and Technology Management, The George Washington University School of Business**

"Tony's book is able to bridge decades of practical experience in complex business settings with systemic and analytical thinking. A very useful and thought-provoking read."
—**Alfonso Fuggetta, CEO and Scientific Director, Cefriel, Politecnico di Milano, Italy**

"Very few leaders have a flawless track record of succeeding consistently with complex digital transformation journeys. Even fewer have articulated the recipe of their success effectively. With this book, Tony has accomplished this rare feat. His rich experience as a practitioner will help digital leaders achieve real results: 10x results, which he defines as one-tenth the cost or ten times the throughput or ten times better user experience. This book is a must-read for leaders navigating every stage of digital transformation."
—**Sanjay Jalona, CEO and Managing Director, LTI**

"It's too late to have a digital strategy; now you need a strategy that includes digital. This book is the most powerful preparation I've seen for leaders in the pervasively digital future."
—**Bob Johansen, Distinguished Fellow, Institute for the Future, and author of** *The New Leadership Literacies*

"A much-needed practitioner's guide that provides invaluable insight and advice on how to tackle probably the most challenging of the 'industrial' revolutions that companies have ever faced."
—**Marek Kapuscinski, former CEO, Procter & Gamble Central Europe, and current supervisory board member, Cyfrowy Polsat SA and Bank Handlowy SA (Citi Handlowy)**

"Tony has the rare ability to take on a complex issue like digital transformation and bring together real-life experience, best-in-class knowledge, and new insights to solve it."
—**Sashi Narahari, cofounder and CEO, HighRadius**

"There are a lot of words and articles on digital transformation but few to show the whole process and blueprint. Tony has succeeded in clarifying where to go with his insights from his excellent career in business transformation. This book is a must-read for business innovators in this world."
—**John Park, founder, Digital Marketing Korea & AI Seoul Summit, and author of** *Data, Platform & Technology Changes the Map of Marketing*

"I have had the pleasure of working with Tony for over twenty years. He has an enviable record of transformations and strategy. I am delighted to see him bring these two together to create a critically important book for leaders."
—**Filippo Passerini, operating executive and former Group President, Global Business Services, and Chief Information Officer, Procter & Gamble**

"The new digital era demands new ways to think about managing change. Tony Saldanha provides a powerful road map with his enviable experience and brilliant insights."
—**Kumar V. Pratap, Joint Secretary (Infrastructure Policy and Finance), Ministry of Finance, Government of India**

"It's one thing for a startup to be born digital. It's another thing entirely for an existing organization to become digital. Tony speaks in plain language and from decades of experience about what a successful digital transformation takes, and, as this book brilliantly illustrates, technology is only part of the answer."
—**Andrew Razeghi, founder, StrategyLab, Inc.; Lecturer, Kellogg School of Management, Northwestern University; author of** *Bend the Curve*; **and active angel investor**

"The Shared Services & Outsourcing Network has long regarded the transformative results from Tony's work with deep respect. It's great to see the formula finally documented in this excellent book."
—**Naomi Secor, Global Managing Director, The Shared Services & Outsourcing Network**

"Tony's book should be required reading for all leaders who are seeking to drive a digital revolution in their company. It provides practical guidance on the discipline needed to make the organization, process, and culture changes that fuel success."
—**Andy Shih, Vice President and General Manager of Digital Commerce, Nike, Greater China**

"Fantastic! This book reveals the root cause of failed digital transformations. If you're an innovative or a progressive leader, you will want to arm yourself with the insights and practical tips offered here."
—**Ed Sim, founder and Managing Partner, Boldstart Ventures**

"As businesses that last for centuries have demonstrated, successful transformation takes vision and disciplined leadership. Tony applies the same principles to today's challenges, showing that digital isn't the problem, it is actually an enabler to help achieve your strategic vision."
—**Mindy Simon, Chief Information Officer, Global Business & Information Services, Conagra**

"This is a must-read for seasoned leaders and novices alike. Tony Saldanha's well-written, pragmatic approach to digital transformation provides a simple road map to succeeding in the digital era."
—**Richard Smullen, founder and CEO, Pypestream**

"If you believe in the disruptive power of digital technology and want to do something about it, then this book is for you."
—**Dr. Venkat Srinivasan, serial entrepreneur and author of *The Intelligent Enterprise in the Era of Big Data***

"Tony is an industry expert who has the credibility of having run large operations, led disruptive innovation, and transformed successful operations into disruptive new models. This book reveals many of his secrets."
—**Sheree Stomberg, Global Head of Citi Shared Services**

"Failure is often more illuminating than deconstructing success because it takes a sharper and tougher prescription. It's with this understanding that Tony casts a hard eye on digital transformation."
—**Paco Underhill, CEO, Envirosell, and author of *Why We Buy***

"Tony Saldanha tells us in simple terms how to thrive in these digitally disruptive times. This is a book no leader can afford to miss."
—**Robert Weltevreden, Head of Novartis Business Services**

Why Digital Transformations Fail

The Surprising Disciplines of How
to Take Off and Stay Ahead

Tony Saldanha

Berrett–Koehler Publishers, Inc.
a BK Business book

Berrett-Koehler Publishers, Inc.
1333 Broadway, Suite 1000
Oakland, CA 94612-1921
Tel: (510) 817-2277
Fax: (510) 817-2278
www.bkconnection.com

ORDERING INFORMATION

Quantity sales. Special discounts are available on quantity purchases by corporations, associations, and others. For details, contact the "Special Sales Department" at the Berrett-Koehler address above.

Individual sales. Berrett-Koehler publications are available through most bookstores. They can also be ordered directly from Berrett-Koehler: Tel: (800) 929-2929; Fax: (802) 864-7626; www.bkconnection.com.

Orders for college textbook / course adoption use. Please contact Berrett-Koehler: Tel: (800) 929-2929; Fax: (802) 864-7626.

Distributed to the U.S. trade and internationally by Penguin Random House Publisher Services.

Berrett-Koehler and the BK logo are registered trademarks of Berrett-Koehler Publishers, Inc.

Printed in Canada

Berrett-Koehler books are printed on long-lasting acid-free paper. When it is available, we choose paper that has been manufactured by environmentally responsible processes. These may include using trees grown in sustainable forests, incorporating recycled paper, minimizing chlorine in bleaching, or recycling the energy produced at the paper mill.

Library of Congress Cataloging-in-Publication Data

Names: Saldanha, Tony, author.
  Title: Why digital transformations fail : the surprising disciplines of how
    to take off and stay ahead / Tony Saldanha.
  Description: First edition. | Oakland, CA : Berrett-Koehler Publishers, 2019.
    | Includes bibliographical references and index.
  Identifiers: LCCN 2019009561 | ISBN 9781523085347 (hardcover : alk paper)
  Subjects: LCSH: Information technology—Management. | Technological
    innovations--Management. | Organizational change. | Strategic planning.
  Classification: LCC HD30.2 .S254 2019 | DDC 004.068--dc23
  LC record available at https://lccn.loc.gov/2019009561

First Edition

24 23 22 21 20 19   10 9 8 7 6 5 4 3 2 1

Interior design and production by Dovetail Publishing Services
Jacket design by Emma Smith

To @saldanhaclan—Ernest, Veronica, Julia, Lara, and Rene. Family doesn't get any better than this.

Contents

Diligence is the mother of good fortune.

—Miguel de Cervantes, *Don Quixote*

Foreword

"Tony, how can Peter Arnett of CNN have a satellite dish in his brief-case to broadcast to the world about the invasion of Iraq and our warehouses can't communicate with our distribution system in the Philippines?" I asked. I became the general manager of our Procter & Gamble operations in the Philippines in mid-1991 after the Gulf War had already begun. The Procter & Gamble Company entered the Philippines through acquisition in 1935. But when I became general manager, we were not delivering on our potential. We had warehouses scattered throughout the seven thousand–plus islands of the Philippines and were unable to ship all orders. Our warehouses couldn't communicate with each other or our factories. In those days it took years to get the Philippine phone company to install a landline, and cell phones were not yet reliable. This is why I challenged our new information technology leader, the author, Tony Saldanha, to use technology to leapfrog the problem.

I have always believed in the competitive advantage benefits of digital technology. I wrote binary-coded decimal (BCD) programs for an IBM 360 computer in high school. At West Point I took every computer software and hardware course available and wrote portions of an assembly program for our Honeywell mainframe computer to translate Fortran IV into BCD. Later, as chief executive officer of the Procter & Gamble Company, I set a path for P&G, according to *Global Intelligence for the CIO* magazine (April–June 2012), to be the first Fortune 50 company to "digitize the company from end to end." McKinsey & Company summed it up as "creating the world's most technologically enabled company." This meant that every individual in the company would have a customized dashboard on their computer that would allow them to view their metrics in real time and drill down as needed, by brand and by country, to understand what was happening and react to create competitive advantage. We called this initiative Project Symphony, and it was led by Tony Saldanha.

You see, the Procter & Gamble Company was rapidly globalizing in the 1980s and 1990s, and I was fortunate enough to be a part of it. Assignments on our biggest brands like Tide; in multiple international locations like Canada, the Philippines, Japan, and Belgium; and across geographies-leading categories or operations all convinced me that technology could provide the competitive advantage to gleaning insights first and expanding them more broadly. Taking advantage of this potential means digitizing before your competition. Today, this seems rather anachronistic. The question is no longer "whether to transform" but more "how to transform." This book by Tony, based on his years of experience and multiple attempts all over the world, provides an important step-by-step guide to improving transformation success rates.

When I became the eighth secretary of the Department of Veterans Affairs, the second largest department in the federal government after the Department of Defense, I faced the same challenge to transform the organization using digital technology. In fact, I became secretary when employees lied to my predecessor and "cooked the books," causing veterans to not get timely health care in Phoenix. My first trip after Senate confirmation was to Phoenix, and I discovered the PC-based system we asked our schedulers to use dated to 1985 and was like operating green-screen MS-DOS. Beyond this, we were managing our more than $185 billion budget using COBOL, a mainframe computer language I coded at West Point in 1972. I hired an individual who had been CIO at Johnson & Johnson and Dell to help me transform the VA via digitization. For example, using human-centered design principles, we created one website for veterans to replace over a thousand disparate sites, most of which required unique usernames and passwords.

Tony's experience has made him an expert on digital transformation. In the Philippines and in Asia he created a new model for digitizing our distributors—dedicated companies that represented our sales and logistics capabilities in situations where the retailers were too small and disparate for P&G employees to serve them directly. As previously noted, he led Project Symphony across the global enterprise as we worked to turn our myriad of data into real-time decision making for time compression competitive advantage. In P&G's Central and Eastern Europe, Middle East, and Africa Division, Tony further perfected the linkages between the corporation and its distributors with a real-time distributor connect initiative. It provided more real-time visibility to store sales and inventory in small stores, for example in

Nigeria, than at Walmart stores in the United States. As Tony moved up the ladder at P&G, he applied his considerable digital transformation skills more broadly across the company.

I wholeheartedly recommend this book to every reader. Tony's three decades worth of deep experience and the use of the airline industry–inspired checklist system is unique. It will prevent you from making the mistakes Tony and I already made, help you beat the odds of the 70 percent failure rate in digital transformations, and enable you to deliver competitive advantage to your enterprise.

Robert A. McDonald

Retired Chairman, President, and Chief Executive Officer,
The Procter & Gamble Company;

Eighth Secretary of the Department of Veterans Affairs

Preface

In the spring of 2015, a Procter & Gamble colleague and close friend, Brent Duersch, and I were just wrapping up a conference call with a top-tier consultancy on how to go about disruptive transformation. As Brent reached across the table to end the call, he chuckled, "Either we're missing something, or none of these guys has actually done true digital transformation." This was our tenth call in three days with organizations that had either undergone a successful major transformation or supposedly had a proven framework on how to do it.

Brent and I were trying to piece together the "how to" methodology for a disruptive transformation of our Global Business Services organization that had to be successful, sustainable, and scalable. We were starting to realize that although there were some nuggets to be gained via these meetings, perhaps we weren't going to find the answer we were looking for.

Four years later, I now realize that our situation then is fairly common in today's world. Executives, business owners, public sector leaders, academics, and even new hires in organizations all fully realize the disruptive power of digital capabilities in today's world. They know that it is the preeminent disruptive threat of our generation, as well as its biggest opportunity. They really want to transform their work and their lives, but the nagging question is, "How?"

Perhaps you're a leader who has invested time, money, and personal credibility into digital transformation already. However, you have a niggling doubt that something is not right, because while you see anecdotal success, it doesn't make much of a dent in your overall business model. Meanwhile, the clock keeps ticking as large-scale disruptions of businesses, industries, societies, and personal lives continue unabated. Iconic names like Sears, Macy's, Neiman Marcus, Tiffany, and Harley-Davidson continue to struggle. It's up to us as leaders to determine whether our organizations succumb or prevail in the opportunity of a lifetime.

I strongly believe that every change is an opportunity, and by that yardstick this is an opportunity of historic proportions. My P&G career of twenty-seven years provided me with vast experiences ranging from digitally transforming sales in parts of Africa to using AI to automate portions of supply chain operations worldwide. It allowed me to be on the leading edge of industry-shaping multibillion-dollar outsourcing deals and on hard-core organizational change programs such as the integration of the $10 billion Gillette company systems into P&G when I was Gillette's chief information officer. These experiences provided a unique foundation for me to tackle how organizations can face up to the biggest change management issue of their lives: transforming the core of their operations into a fully digital backbone.

So, rather than get discouraged by the lack of good insights from our meetings, Brent and I would double down on them. We would meet more than one hundred entities over the next couple of months, including industry analysts, strategic partners, research institutions, universities, peer companies, VCs, accelerators, and more. Mixing the nuggets from these with our firsthand P&G experience gained over time, some clear insights would emerge. First, there are different shades of transformations possible, and you need to be diligent in targeting a complete and sustainable transformation during these disruptive times. Second, the surprising reason why as many as 70 percent of all digital transformations fail is a lack of discipline. And third, it is possible to apply proven failure-reduction approaches, like the disciplined checklist model from the aviation industry, to significantly improve the odds of success in digital transformation.

If you're a business leader, a business owner, an executive, or a manager of people; if you work in corporate settings, in government, in academia, or in the nonprofit sector; if you believe that digital transformation is the ultimate challenge of our generation and that the issue is not "whether" but "how"; if you're interested in hearing about how other organizations and people across generations tackled this issue, then this book will interest you.

As my journey through P&G's digital transformation of its shared services unfurled after 2015, Brent kept joking that I should perhaps document our approach. "Write a book!" he said. I found that amusing. "Me?" I said. "I'm never going to write a book."

I may have been premature about that.

How to Read This Book

This book is meant for anyone who fully appreciates the urgency of digital transformation and is interested in beating the dismal odds of success on this topic. It will help you set the correct end goal for digital transformation, where digital becomes the "living DNA" of your enterprise. Additionally, it will provide you a disciplined checklist approach on exactly how to get there.

The structure of the book mimics the five-stage model of maturity for digital transformation. Part I sets the stage, first by describing the dilemma faced by P&G's Global Business Services to drive perpetual digital transformation, then by introducing the five-stage digital transformation model and the specific checklist steps that can be used to deliver success. Following this, part II explores the five stages of digital transformation in detail. For each stage, two chapters describe the two most important disciplines necessary for success. Finally, part III demonstrates how all these disciplines can be assembled together to address the threat of the Fourth Industrial Revolution systemically.

My ultimate goal is to provide practical, tested, and reliable tools and ideas on how to thrive on digital transformation. There are a couple of resources available at the end of the book, "Checklist of the Surprising Disciplines" and "How to Use the Five Most Exponential Technologies," that I think you'll find helpful. However, the form and size of the book itself is a limitation. I invite you to visit my website www.tonysaldanha.com, where further examples, tools, and materials are available, in addition to information on how to contact me for follow-up.

Part I

Why Digital Transformations Fail and What to Do about It

Chapter 1

How to Survive an Industrial Revolution

"I hate shopping!" I muttered to myself as I stood gazing with horror at the shuttered Macy's store in downtown Cincinnati, my hometown. To be clear, I dislike shopping even at the best of times. However, this event was a thousand times worse. Perhaps you recall Indiana Jones's expression in Raiders of the Lost Ark *when he throws his torch into the Well of Souls in anticipation of climbing down, only to find that the floor is moving because it is covered with thousands of snakes. "Snakes," he says. "Why'd it have to be snakes?" I suspect my face wore that exact same stricken expression that day. In the movie, Sallah, Indiana's sidekick, adds unhelpfully, "Asps. Very dangerous. You go first." That's usually my approach to shopping when I nudge my wife forward, who equally dislikes the chore.*

I couldn't use the "I'm right behind you" approach that day. I was on a mission to buy her a gift for a major anniversary, which was on that day. For a change I had the whole gift-buying stuff under control, or so I thought. We had come across the gift I had in mind during a previous expedition to the downtown Cincinnati Macy's. I knew she liked it. To make matters worse, I had even dropped some hints that this would be the anniversary gift. Today was D-day, and I had planned to pick it up on my way home.

Except that when I reached the store, it was closed. As in, closed forever. I faintly recalled the announcement a few months earlier that the Cincinnati downtown location would be among the hundred-plus stores Macy's planned to shut down in the US. Now, hoping that other retailers would have the gift I needed, I frantically searched online. It was available, except that in today's omnichannel world, it was not stocked in the physical stores. I would have to order it online and then visit the store to pick it up, but not for five business days. "Guaranteed on-time delivery" the website promised. As if that helped me with my last-minute shopping!

3

As I drove home with the printout of the order representing the anniversary gift, I pondered the irony of the "retail apocalypse,"[1] a term coined by the media to describe the mass closing of brick-and-mortar retail stores in North America, coming back to bite one of the few people who had hitherto been totally indifferent to it.

Retail Apocalypse: A Symptom of the Fourth Industrial Revolution

The real estate firm Cushman & Wakefield has estimated that twelve thousand retail stores will have closed in 2018 in the US, up from nine thousand in 2017. That includes several iconic chains that filed for bankruptcy, including Sears, Mattress Factory, Brookstone, Rockport, Southeastern Grocers, Nine West, and Bon-Ton in 2018.[2] That's on top of names such as Toys "R" Us, Payless ShoeSource, hhgregg, the Limited, Aéropostale, Sports Authority, and Radio Shack in the previous two years. The retail sector continues to be among the top of the list of bankruptcies in the US along with the energy sector. Investopedia has called 2018 the year of retail bankruptcies.[3]

The retail sector is one of several industries being disrupted in the US and around the world. As we all know, media, telecom, hospitality, automotive, financial, health care, consumer products, education, manufacturing, and logistics are being affected, and they are not the only ones either. Zoom out further and you see a broader trend altering how we live, work, and communicate. That's the Fourth Industrial Revolution.

The Fourth Industrial Revolution has digital technology transforming and fusing together the physical, biological, chemical, and information worlds. It's a force for massive new opportunity in every area valued by society—everything from convenience (e.g., online shopping) and improved health (e.g., biotech) to personal security (e.g., digital homes), food security (e.g., agrotech), and so on. Digital technology frees workers from tedious tasks, allowing them the opportunity to migrate to higher value-added responsibilities. As with any new powerful technology, there is indeed the potential for destructive applications (e.g., weaponry, designer babies, loss of privacy, playing to humanity's worst impulses on social media). To what degree the good prevails over the bad is up to us, and it is currently unknown. However, one thing is guaranteed: it will bring about dramatic change. As with the prior three industrial revolutions, individuals and societies will be affected significantly, and companies will either transform or die. That's where this book comes in.

How to Thrive in an Industrial Revolution

This book is about understanding why digital transformations fail as a means to a more important end, which is how to thrive in an industrial revolution. It builds upon five major foundations to do this:

- Companies either transform or die in industrial revolutions.

- Digital transformation is our current generation's attempt to transform in the face of the Fourth Industrial Revolution.

- As many as 70 percent of all digital transformations fail.

- The surprising answer to why digital transformations fail is a lack of discipline in defining *and* executing the right steps for digital transformations to take off and stay ahead.

- It is possible to apply the proven checklist methodology from the airline and medical fields to improve the 70 percent failure rate.

The battle to thrive in the Fourth Industrial Revolution isn't going to be easy, but it is possible. We can certainly do much better than the current 70 percent failure rate,[4,5] as I have learned from my Procter & Gamble experience. The goal is worth it. At stake is not just the existential threat to individual companies and their employees but the power to shape products, influence employee and consumer self-worth, uplift societies, and leave the world in a much better place than when we started. To get going, let's elaborate on the foundations mentioned above.

Industry Turbulence Happens during All Industrial Revolutions

The current turbulence in retail and other industries is a classic trend during an industrial revolution. It has happened in prior industrial revolutions, although the technology drivers of change were different. Companies die during industrial revolutions. Obviously, they don't die without a fight. Their demise often occurs despite the best efforts of reputable, visionary, and innovative leaders to transform their companies. This has been true of prior industrial revolutions as well, as we will see later in this chapter. A few are successful, but unfortunately most are not.

70 Percent of All Digital Transformations Fail

As mentioned earlier, digital transformation is the modern-day fight to survive the existential threat of digital disruption caused by the Fourth Industrial Revolution. Half the companies on the Fortune 500 list will turn over in the next decade. The disruption is here, it's massive, and it's urgent. Per Credit Suisse,[6] the average life span of an S&P 500 company today is twenty years, down from sixty years in the 1950s, and falling fast. Entrepreneurs, boards, executives, and public organizations are actively consumed by this issue. However, the sad truth is that 70 percent of all digital transformations still fail today. Some have put that number as high as 84 percent.[7] That's a shocking number, given the extremely high stakes. We must do better!

Why Language Gets in the Way of Successful Digital Transformation

This explosive mix of a highly disruptive era and low transformation success rates in today's world is fascinating. Part of the issue is terminology. Most people don't realize that digital disruption *is* the Fourth Industrial Revolution. The term "digital" is very broad. We wore digital watches in the 1970s, and we have had digital telephones and thermometers for a few decades. Isn't digital transformation old news?

To bring stronger definition to the term "digital transformation," we need to frame it in the context of the broader change affecting our lives via the concept of industrial revolutions.

- *First Industrial Revolution*: The evolution of society in the eighteenth and nineteenth centuries from mostly agrarian to industrial and urban, which was mostly driven by mechanical innovations such as the steam engine.
- *Second Industrial Revolution*: The explosive growth of industries from the late 1800s to the First World War. This was driven by mass-production techniques, electric power, and the internal combustion engine.
- *Third Industrial Revolution*: The widespread change beginning in the 1980s with PCs and the internet, due to new electronic technologies.
- *Fourth Industrial Revolution*: The melding of the physical, digital, and biological worlds today. The major driver is the availability of

massive computing capacity at negligible and further plummeting costs. Thus, what used to be physical (e.g., retail stores) can be digital (e.g., online shopping), or what used to be purely biological (e.g., traditional medicine) can be biotech (e.g., personalized genetic medication).

Within this context, the terms "digital disruption" and "digital transformation" become easy to define.

- *Digital disruption*: The effect of the Fourth Industrial Revolution in the corporate and public sector landscapes. Increasingly pervasive and inexpensive digital technology is causing widespread industrial, economic, and social change. This explosive change has occurred only in the past decade or two.

- *Digital transformation*: The migration of enterprises and societies from the Third to the Fourth Industrial Revolution era. For companies, this means having digital technology become the backbone of new products and services, new ways of operation, and new business models.

Armed with this definition of digital transformation, we can now go back to previous industrial revolutions for lessons on why transformations fail in general.

The Inability of the John Stephenson Company to Take Off on Its Transformation

The venerable John Stephenson Company was a leading player in the carriage industry that died in the Second Industrial Revolution. It wasn't alone; very few carriage companies survived that era. The metamorphosis of the transportation industry from carriages to automobiles is one of the best-documented case studies of the Second Industrial Revolution and therefore serves up several fascinating insights.

The horse and carriage industry wasn't just the personal transportation sector in the 1800s; it was the underpinning of industrial transportation (i.e., goods), information communication (e.g., moving newspapers and mail), and ancillary industries (e.g., horse feed). In 1880, Brooklyn and Manhattan alone had 249 carriage makers.[8] Its disruption would be a major event.

In the 1890s, Times Square in New York was *the* place for carriage sale and repair. Blacksmiths vied for your attention, right next to carriage stores. In 1914 there were an estimated 4,600 carriage companies in the United States. In the next eleven years, that number had plunged to only 150![9] Unfortunately, the John Stephenson Company wasn't among the survivors.

John G. Stephenson had started his business in 1831. Over the next several decades, his business rapidly expanded to make carriages, omnibuses (multiseated carriage buses drawn by horses), wagons, streetcars (carriages run on rail lines), and even gun carriages and pontoons during the Civil War. His carriages were sold in the UK, Mexico, Cuba, South America, Europe, Eastern Russia, Japan, and the East Indies. As with any enterprise, the John Stephenson Company's business ebbed and flowed with the economy, but under Stephenson's determined leadership it maintained a stronghold in the carriage market—that is, until the end of the century, when the transportation industry itself entered a turbulent era during the Second Industrial Revolution. The company went into voluntary bankruptcy. It was acquired in 1904 by the J. G. Brill Company of Philadelphia. That didn't last either. Finally, in August of 1919, the Stephenson plant was sold and the company liquidated.

There are several lessons served up by the efforts of companies like the John Stephenson Company to stave off disruption during an industrial revolution. Their demise may have been caused by a different technology (i.e., piston engines, not digital), but failed transformations during any industrial revolution have several things in common.

For instance, the death of the John Stephenson Company helps us distinguish between successful innovators within *current* business models, and transformations to *new* models during industrial revolutions. Stephenson was very innovative within the carriage industry. He built the first streetcar that ran on rails in the US. There are at least eighteen patents attributed to him. His company innovated successfully in its operations and its products several times, from horse-drawn omnibuses, to horse-drawn carriages that ran on rails, to electric streetcars. Ultimately, the issue wasn't the John Stephenson Company's ability to innovate within the carriage industry era; it was its *inability* to transform to the internal combustion engine era. There was never a disciplined transformational effort to evolve from the carriage industry to the automobile industry.

Transformation during industrial revolutions demands a different game plan than innovation within the current business model.

For an industrial revolution–driven transformation to take off, you need a different, disciplined, new business model game plan. This was a recurring issue in the failure of most carriage companies. Having said that, *creating* a new game plan for a different business model is just the price of entry. The disciplined *execution* of this new game plan is equally important, as I illustrate with the next story.

Studebaker's Inability to Sustain Its Transformation

For most collectors of classic cars, Studebaker holds a very special place. Studebaker cars were the Apple products of their era—distinctive in their designs, excellent in their quality, and perhaps even more valuable for the money than Apple is today. The 1950s Studebaker cars are still considered to be among the best automobiles in history!

Studebaker was also the only large carriage company that directly transitioned successfully from carriage making into automobiles.

The Studebaker Corporation had an engineer working on an automobile as early as 1897. It is known to have manufactured both automobiles and wagons in the early 1900s. The company experimented with both electric- and gas-powered cars and eventually settled on the latter. Wagon production ended in 1920,[10] and the Studebaker Corporation focused on automobiles alone after that.

But as we know, Studebaker doesn't make any cars today. Although Studebaker had clearly transformed into the automobile era and arguably had the best products, it never mastered the business model for scale and sustainable profit margins. Studebaker continued to build cars until the 1960s. Its plant in Hamilton, Ontario, Canada, closed in 1966, finally ending a 114-year history of Studebaker vehicles.

Studebaker was able to move into the automobile industry but not win within it. There wasn't a long-term plan for scaling to provide ongoing viable value propositions to its customers. For instance, its board consistently chose to pay big dividends to shareholders instead of reinvesting in modernizing its factories.[11] Their competitors at GM and Ford were much more aggressive in both operational efficiencies as well as pricing and therefore prevailed.[12]

True transformation must include building capabilities to stay ahead of your competition long term.

Successful transformation during an industrial revolution is good, but sustainable market leaders need to go a step further. They need to sustain the business model. The transformation is incomplete if the new business model cannot be built with an eye toward perpetual evolution.

How to Take Off *and* Stay Ahead During an Industrial Revolution

The John Stephenson Company's transformation failed to take off, while the Studebaker Corporation failed to stay ahead. In the long run, it's only the ability of an enterprise to reach a Zen-like state of perpetual innovation leadership, which I call "Stage 5" digital transformation, that matters. The five-stage digital transformation model will be developed further in the coming chapters, and it is the organizing structure of this book itself, along with the disciplines to deliver successful transformations. For the moment, it's sufficient to emphasize the importance of deliberate goal setting for Stage 5 transformation or perpetual winning as the most desirable outcome of any transformation. A one-time successful transformation is insufficient to weather the repeated disruptions that occur within each industrial revolution. Distinguishing between transformation *takeoff* and *staying ahead* is key.

- *Transformation takeoff*: This is the tipping point for successful operation of the enterprise from one generation of the industrial revolution to the next. Using an airplane analogy, the operating model of the enterprise takes off from one state (on the ground) to another (flight). The John Stephenson Company failed at this stage.

- *Staying ahead*: Building on the flight analogy, a successful takeoff must be followed by sustained flight. Studebaker failed to achieve the state of staying ahead. Achieving this penultimate stage of success is fine for a short while, but it does not guarantee ongoing survival during times of rapid change. The issue is that you are one technology or one product or one business-environmental change away from being disrupted.

There are two ways in which digital transformations fail. The lack of discipline causes them to first, fail to take off, and second, to maintain momentum, and they end up crashing.

Both challenges were uppermost in my mind in 2015 when I took on the challenge of deliberately disrupting Procter & Gamble's best-in-class Global Business Services unit.

Applying Successful Transformation to Procter & Gamble's Global Business Services

It was early 2015, and I had been with the iconic Procter & Gamble Company for twenty-four years. As a vice president in the multi-billion-dollar Global Business Services (GBS) organization, I had been fortunate to participate over the years in the formation of P&G's industry-leading GBS. A GBS organization provides scaled operations ranging from human resources, finance, manufacturing systems, marketing and sales systems, and information technologies to all business units globally. P&G's GBS was significantly ahead of most peer organizations, and we had influenced the formation of the global business services industry itself, but that was no guarantee of winning in the Fourth Industrial Revolution. The next chapter will cover the circumstances that led to the decision to proactively disrupt ourselves and our approach toward it. That experience led to the insights on how to execute successful digital transformation.

From the outset, the biggest question in my mind was how to execute a transformation that would be ongoing or perpetual. There had been a couple of prior attempts at driving disruptive innovation in GBS. These had resulted in some great innovations, but never at a level that drove perpetual scaled transformation of the entire unit. Our attempt had to be successful in both taking off as well as staying ahead.

The Surprising Answer on How to Take Off and Stay Ahead on Digital Transformations

That challenge to scale innovations with excellence led me to a fascinating insight. I happen to be fascinated by airplanes; OK, I'm an airplane geek, truth be told. I noticed that the planned stages for successful digital transformation of P&G's Global Business Services division would be like the steps needed to complete a successful aircraft takeoff.

Much as I'd like to think that this is a unique, brilliant insight, reality suggests otherwise. A few months ago, I was introduced to Dr. Atul Gawande's seminal book *The Checklist Manifesto: How to Get Things Right*. His work has helped the health-care industry reduce errors significantly. Dr. Gawande's premise was spot-on—a checklist drives repeatable success in complex endeavors. I realized that the disciplined approach to reducing failures by applying the airline checklist model to another field wasn't a novel idea. On the other hand, this was strong validation that it could be done in the digital transformation area.

The surprising answer to delivering perpetual transformation was *discipline*—in both taking off and staying ahead.

In the three years that followed the launch of the GBS change initiative, it became crystal clear that the answer to the issue of perpetual digital transformation would be disciplined execution. The solution for solving the reliability issues in the airline and more recently medical industries also held true for reducing the failure rates of digital transformation.

This makes logical sense. According to *The Economist* magazine, 99.999999 percent[13] of aircraft takeoffs are successful, while only 30 percent of digital transformations can claim success. Are digital transformation efforts inherently more complex in the sense that they involve more judgment? Absolutely! On the other hand, the 99.999999 percent success rate on takeoffs was a mere pipe dream when the aviation industry was in its infancy. A ton of hard work went in over the decades to structure what were judgment-based tasks into simpler routines. Various technologies were applied to automate many of those tasks. And what was not automated has been check-listed to deliver predictable execution.

In Closing

There is little doubt that the Fourth Industrial Revolution will dramatically shift the landscape of industry, just as previous industrial revolutions did. History has proved that the organizations that get disrupted aren't necessarily caught unawares. As with the John Stephenson Company and Studebaker, organizations often see it coming. They are perhaps even successful at transforming themselves once or twice. But they eventually fail to have their transformations either take off or stay ahead. The underlying cause of why 70 percent of digital transformations fail is a lack of sufficient discipline. There's insufficient rigor in both digital transformation takeoff as well as in staying ahead.

This can be addressed by a disciplined checklist approach—influenced by the same methodology that's been successfully applied in the airline industry and the medical field. To execute the checklist approach, the book will lay out a five-stage road map for success in digital transformation, which is defined as the ability to win in the Fourth Industrial Revolution.

Chapter 2

The Disciplines to Move Up to Stage 5 Transformation

It was January of 2015 and Julio Nemeth, the newly minted president of Global Business Services at Procter & Gamble, mulled over an ironic problem. He was taking over an organization that was, by all external benchmarks, already best in class in the shared services industry. His predecessor, Filippo Passerini, had left behind an enviable, globally awarded Global Business Services organization, which had shaped the GBS industry itself along the way.

Nemeth's problem was simple—how to further improve a business model that was already industry leading. The external consultant advice to him was to do "more of the same" since the current P&G model obviously worked brilliantly. Being an innovator, though, he knew that disrupting from a position of strength is always preferable to resting on your laurels.

Shared Services Industry Context

To better understand Nemeth's dilemma, it would help to digress briefly into the shared services industry and, by extension, into Global Business Services at P&G.

Shared services is a construct that allows an enterprise to drive efficiencies of scale by sharing internal services like finance and accounting, supply chain management, HR systems, IT services, or customer relationship management across the enterprise. The shared services unit becomes an internal service provider to other business units within the enterprise and is held accountable to deliver services at significantly improved cost, quality, and timeliness. The usual strategies employed are to sweep together similar services across business units in the enterprise (e.g., payroll), then simplify, standardize, centralize, and automate those processes.

The Evolution of Shared Services

Over the past thirty years, most shared services organizations have evolved through three stages. The usual starting point is piecemeal shared services, where a limited set of services (e.g., only finance and accounting) or a limited geography is available. With maturity, this evolves to the second stage of global or full shared services, where all types of services and all geographies are optimized. The third stage of maturity is global business services, where the shared services organization becomes not just a lower-cost "service provider" to the business but also a proactive transformation agent of the enterprise. This is done by taking on stronger governance functions (e.g., defining process standards across all business units), spearheading business transformation services (e.g., helping other business units digitize), and generating top-line value (e.g., using analytics to grow sales).

P&G's Global Business Services unit had reached the third stage of maturity more than a decade ago. It was extremely wide in its scope, possibly one of the widest in the world. It provided about 160 "services" to P&G's business units across more than a hundred countries. For instance, a "service" could be buildings and facilities management or payroll or sales business analytics. These services were grouped into "service lines" such as IT Services, Financial Shared Services, Supply Chain Shared Services, and so on.

The Fourth Industrial Revolution Applies to Shared Services Too

Nemeth wasn't convinced that the shared services industry's maturity stages ought to stop at three. Knowing the disruptive power of the digital revolution, he wondered if it was possible to create a new fourth stage of evolution of GBS. This would apply not just to P&G but to the entire industry. He pulled me into the effort, and together we created the Next Generation Services (NGS) organization to find and execute this next big disruption for shared services.

At the time, I had worked for twenty-four years at Procter & Gamble. Over this period, I had been privileged to live in six countries, work in a dozen P&G roles, and manage P&G's GBS and IT for all regions of the world. I was delighted with the opportunity to transform the GBS model itself.

Inventing the Next Generation of Shared Services

We started with a simple question: Why should the technology-driven disruptive forces that were acting upon just about every industry not disrupt the shared services industry? If anything, the shared services functions should have been disrupted faster and deeper, given that they were comprised of essentially information and data operations (e.g., accounting, payroll, IT, etc.).

Four years into the digital transformation journey, we know for a fact that there is indeed a fourth stage. Through the work my NGS team did at P&G, we created and implemented several 10X internal operations products (i.e., products that deliver ten times better top line, bottom line, or employee-centric capabilities). Along the journey, we captured a ton of learning on leading successful digital transformations. What we accomplished initially by intuition and trial and error was soon codified. All these lessons are the basis of the surprising disciplines of how to take off and stay ahead during a digital transformation.

However, back in 2015, the GBS digital transformation to the next stage was merely a hypothesis. We searched externally for evidence that this could be proved or disproved. That led us to Salim Ismail, founding executive director and "dean" of Singularity University and author of *Exponential Organizations*.[14]

Exponential Organizations as a Possible End State for GBS

Around the time that we were searching to create the next stage of evolution of shared services, P&G's GBS leadership team had been exposed to a talk by Salim at Singularity University on the topic of exponential organizations. Founded in 2008 by Peter Diamandis and Ray Kurzweil, Singularity University (SU) is, in my opinion, the world's foremost think tank on how disruptive technologies, from artificial intelligence to biotech, can change the world. Salim has since moved on from SU, but he and I still firmly believe that no forward-thinking leader can afford to miss the opportunity to visit SU to learn about how dramatically their business can change.

Salim's pitch was simultaneously mind-blowing and terrifying. He talked about the exponential pace of change, driven by a new generation of technologies. The worrying part of the discussion was the realization of just how near these new disruptions were. It reinforced our belief that GBS had to evolve, and fast.

Salim did more than just scare the living daylights out of his audience. He also offered great insights on an end state, based on his book, *Exponential Organizations,* of what these future organizations might look like. This provided an important jigsaw puzzle piece. P&G's Global Business Services had to transform into an exponential organization. We decided to hire Salim to help create Next Generation Services—the next evolution of Global Business Services.

How Exponential Organizations Can Change the World

Salim defines an exponential organization as one whose impact (or output) is disproportionally large—at least ten times larger—compared to its peers because of the use of new organizational techniques that leverage exponential technologies. Organizations with exponential characteristics and mindsets are in the best position to thrive in the coming digital era. That's because unlike traditional command-and-control organizations, exponential organizations are digital, information-based agencies. Where traditional companies are driven by scarcity of the resources that are under their control, exponential organizations thrive on abundance by tapping the larger ecosystem. Traditional organizations move deliberately. Exponential organizations are flexible, adaptable, and agile and have few barriers to enter any industry and therefore grow explosively.

Why Exponential Organizations Are Necessary

Although we intellectually understand the transformative power of exponential technologies, it's easy to overlook how near the threat is and just how much it can affect enterprises.

Here are a few examples:

- The computing power that is available per $1,000 continues to grow exponentially. By 2023, you will be able to buy the processing capability of an entire human brain! Given the complexity of a human brain, this is a huge landmark.

- A short twenty years after that, you will get the computing capacity of all the human brains on earth for $1,000. Imagine how that might change organization staffing.

- In March 2018, IBM unveiled the world's tiniest computer, which would be one millimeter big and would cost a few cents to manufacture. The University of Michigan responded in June 2018 with their version, which would be a tenth that size.

- The current version of Google's game-playing AI, named Alpha-Zero, taught itself how to play chess in four hours and defeated the world's best chess program, Stockfish 8, by 100 to 0. It had previously beaten the world's best Go players as AlphaGo.

This is highly relevant to enterprise operations. Imagine if manufacturers could throw in an inexpensive tiny computer into every product they sell. What would that do to their supply chain efficiency from supplier to customer? Or think of the possibilities of a self-learning AI program rapidly training itself on complex financial, customer, logistical, medical, or legal issues to make decisions that currently require human "judgment." What would be the future of the workplace if you could buy the capacity of all the world's human brains? Or how would the operation of any enterprise change if blockchain, the currently "unhackable" platform, could connect and enable error-free transactions across all suppliers, customers, and peers at an amazingly low cost?

Creating the Next Generation of Shared Services Products Is Possible

Within days, we had set up Next Generation Services and reached out externally to learn about 10X idea possibilities from more than a hundred organizations—consultancies, peer companies, venture capitalists, start-ups, educational institutions, and futurists. The next month was a roller-coaster ride that was both thrilling and terrifying, with periodically stomach-churning jolts of new digital reality that had us questioning whether the digital revolution wasn't even *more* urgent than we had thought.

One such experience occurred in April 2015. I was trying to schedule a meeting over email with AJ Brustein, the CEO of a start-up named Wonolo. I sent AJ an email message suggesting that a P&G colleague and I would be open to a phone call. AJ responded, "Sounds great. Copying Amy as well. Thanks." He copied Amy Ingram, who I assumed was his assistant. This was on April 10, a Friday. To clarify availability, I replied to him and Amy, "Thanks AJ, I am out next week, but perhaps we can connect the following week?" and copied my admin assistant Kim on the message. Later that day, we got a message from Amy: "Happy to get something on AJ's calendar. Does Monday, Apr 20 at 11:00am PDT work? Alternatively, AJ is available on Monday, Apr 20 at 4:00pm PDT or Tuesday, Apr 21 at 10:00am. I'll include the dial-in on the invite." Kim chose a time over email, and the meeting was all set. It was just a routine day at the office. However, later that day, a P&G colleague copied on the messages asked me to check out Amy's digital signature on her email. It said, "Amy Ingram | Personal Assistant to AJ. Brustein" and below that, "x.ai—artificial intelligence that schedules meetings." Amy was a robot!

I was flabbergasted! This was a "Turing test" type moment for me—the test, named after Alan Turing in 1950, being a challenge of a machine's capability to exhibit intelligent behavior that's indistinguishable from a human's. We dissected Amy's responses carefully. Her messages were in perfect business language. "She" had clearly "read" and "understood" my email on April 10 that I wouldn't be available the next week and had therefore suggested times on April 20 and 21.

If a robot could manage the most personal type of executive service, then why couldn't AI run so-called "judgment-based" financial decisions with suppliers and customers on accounts receivables and payables? Why could we not supplement our buyers in the purchases function with an AI "buddy" that could digest the latest information on suppliers, materials, pricing trends, and payments and trigger advice and decisions? Could we not redefine the traditional corporate systems user experience from Stone Age to Siri? Could we perhaps forecast and proactively self-heal most IT systems outages across the P&G globe? Could algorithms replan our supply chain in real time?

The game was on! However, there was one little question we had to deal with next: How exactly would we do this?

A Road Map for Digital Transformation

That question in early 2015 is not too different from the situation faced by most executives, entrepreneurs, and public sector leaders today. How do you go about achieving successful digital transformation? It is certainly a top priority for most CEOs based on a study by the Economist Intelligence Unit.[15] Another study by Gartner[16] says that half the CEOs expect their industry to be substantially or unrecognizably transformed by digital. The issue is no longer whether to transform but how to go about it. And frustration is building as the gap between understanding the criticality of digital transformation and actual results of successful transformations widens.

P&G and GBS had a long history of experience with disruptive innovation. We knew that the odds of true digital transformation to an ongoing perpetual stage of innovation tend to be low. We had heard about the 70 percent failure rates in digital transformation and had previously experienced some of this pain.

What we needed was a road map. Something that we could use to clearly articulate and measure successful digital transformation as well as walk us step-by-step through the journey. Over time, we created such a road map. Disciplined execution inspired by the airline checklist methodology was built into it. This was the operating model for NGS.

To date, this has been highly successful in delivering disruptive outcomes, been reapplied through more than twenty-five disruptive innovation experiments (projects) at NGS, and fine-tuned over time. (Disruptive projects were called "experiments" in NGS, as part of a new language for smart risk-taking.) Though the model has evolved significantly with experience over time, it essentially provided us the rigorous disciplines (checklist steps) to deliver success (i.e., achieve Stage 5 transformation).

The Five-Stage Digital Transformation Model

Recall that we defined digital transformation in chapter 1 as the migration of organizations from the Third Industrial Revolution to the Fourth. The chapter also demonstrated that to thrive in periods of industrial revolutions, the transformation must help the organization to both take off and stay ahead. Therefore, the only logical end point of successful digital transformations must be to reach the stage of perpetual market leadership via innovation. This is Stage 5 digital transformation.

Locking in the right definition of digital transformation also helps cut through the hype of technology vendors and consultants who tend to brand their offerings as "digital transformation." The five-stage digital transformation model in figure 1 is an easy way to distinguish between in-process stages and the end stage.

Stage 1 is the *Foundation*. This is where enterprises are actively automating internal processes, such as selling, manufacturing, or finance, using SAP, Oracle, Salesforce, or similar platforms. This is more automation (also called digitalization) than transformation, but it provides the digitalized foundation necessary for future transformation. Automating processes using digital platforms is necessary to convert manual effort into data.

The next stage is called *Siloed*, where you might see *individual* functions or businesses start to use disruptive technologies to create new business models. So for instance, the manufacturing function may have made progress on using the Internet of Things to drive major changes in the way they manufacture or manage logistics, or the finance manager may have heard about blockchain and transformed the way they do intercompany accounting across countries. Alternatively, a business unit within the enterprise may have used technology to create a completely new business model, such as selling direct to consumer as opposed to via retailers. The point is that these efforts are siloed, and there is no overall company strategy driving transformation.

Stage 3 is *Partially Synchronized* transformation. The enterprise leader, owner, or CEO has recognized the disruptive power of digital technologies and defined a digital future state. At Stage 3, the organization has started rowing in the same direction. However, the enterprise has not completed transforming to a digital backbone or new business models, nor has the agile, innovative culture become sustainable. A good example of this is GE's digital transformation, which ultimately stalled at this stage. CEO Jeff Immelt defined his vision for a digital industrial future. The entire firm started to move toward a single digital strategy. However, the new digital business model never matured enough to develop strong roots.

Stage 4, *Fully Synchronized*, marks the point where an enterprise-wide digital platform or new business model has fully taken root. However, it is a one-time transformation. It is still just one technology (or business model) change away from being disrupted. The only way to survive continuous disruption threats is to make digital capabilities and an agile innovative culture an ongoing integral part of the enterprise.

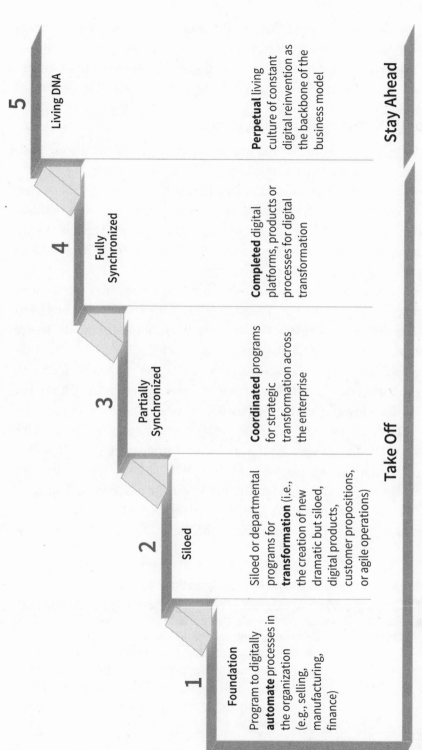

Figure 1 The five-stage digital transformation model

1

Foundation

Program to digitally **automate** processes in the organization (e.g., selling, manufacturing, finance)

2

Siloed

Siloed or departmental programs for **transformation** (i.e., the creation of new dramatic but siloed, digital products, customer propositions, or agile operations)

3

Partially Synchronized

Coordinated programs for strategic transformation across the enterprise

4

Fully Synchronized

Completed digital platforms, products or processes for digital transformation

5

Living DNA

Perpetual living culture of constant digital reinvention as the backbone of the business model

Take Off

Stay Ahead

Stage 5, or *Living DNA*, is the step where the transformation becomes perpetual. You maintain ongoing industry trend leadership because you are disciplined in constantly innovating and setting industry trends. You're not just a market leader; you're a disciplined innovator.

Doing Digital vs. Becoming Digital

How to transform an existing organization can be an exhausting challenge, especially given the immense power of digital technologies. Digital technologies can enable so many things. Should you go after a new business model? Or try a new idea extension of your current business model? Perhaps you should pursue a digitally enabled version of your existing business? The conventional wisdom here is to create a separate digital strategy to answer these questions.

My experience shows that this is a mistake. Instead, I recommend redoing your current business strategy to fully transform using digital capabilities. The distinction is more than subtle. It's the difference between "doing" digital and "becoming" digital. This goal of "becoming" digital is key to achieving perpetual digital transformation. An organization can "do" digital as part of a one-time transformation, but to achieve ongoing market leadership it needs to "become" digital.

The organization has reached the "become" stage when digital is the "living DNA" of its operation. A new digital strategy may deliver a one-time Stage 4 transformation, but it is unlikely to get you to an ongoing Stage 5 transformation. At Stage 5, the enterprise has "become" digital.

A useful way to distinguish between the five stages of transformation is to think of what each stage is *not*. Table 1 illustrates this.

Table 1 Digital transformation: What you are doing and what you are not doing

Stages	What You Are Doing	What You Are Not
1. Foundation	You're upgrading your technology to the latest digital platforms, including cloud, AI, etc. You're "digitalizing" your operations. And seeing huge "scale" benefits.	You're not "transforming." You have no digitally disruptive products, customer relations, or operations.

Stages	What You Are Doing	What You Are Not
2. Siloed	Parts of your organization are experimenting with transformational business models and products. This is on top of the scaled automation of Stage 1.	There is no enterprise-wide strategy to completely transform your business model itself.
3. Partially Synchronized	Your enterprise has a mix of old and new digital business models, processes, and products. All are following a corporate-wide strategy.	You are not fully invested in a full transformation or capable of fending off nimble "digitally native" competition.
4. Fully Synchronized	You're delivering industry-leading customer results, innovative digital products, and best-in-class operational efficiency.	You're not winning perpetually. You're digitally optimized for the moment. But you are one technology, product, or process change away from being disrupted again.
5. Living DNA	Digital operation is your DNA. You are the ultimate ever-evolving market leader. You operate fully digitally. Your workforce is digitally savvy. You provide hugely personalized creative value to customers. You have the most innovative business model. And your transformation is fully synchronized and ongoing. You maintain ongoing industry trend leadership with disciplined innovation. You're a step beyond being a market leader; you're a disciplined market leader constantly leveraging digital.	You're not static. Your enterprise morphs constantly to stay ahead of competition.

Ways to Get to Stage 5

The Digital Transformation 5.0 model provides a road map. As with any road map, there is a sequence of steps that cannot be skipped. However, the journey can certainly be expedited, and some steps can be combined for a leapfrogging effect.

Figure 2 calls out the different options to get to Stage 5. Traditional organizations desiring digital transformation will start at any stage from 1 to 4 and can either slowly *evolve* or rapidly *leapfrog* to Stage 5, which is the ongoing desirable plateau. On the other hand, successful digitally native organizations have a starting advantage in that they already have

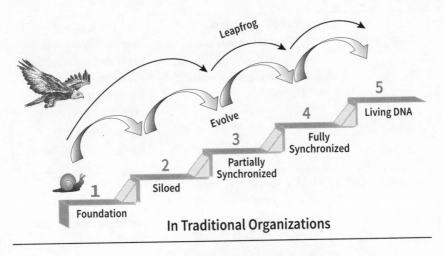

In Traditional Organizations

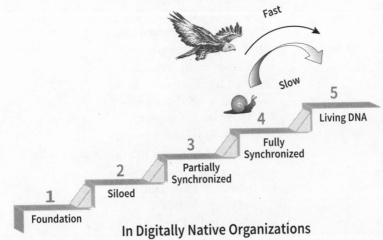

In Digitally Native Organizations

Figure 2 Ways to get to Stage 5

a synchronized digital platform to start with. However, they also need to move up to Stage 5.

Unless your organization happens to be a successful "digitally native" organization—i.e., a company that started with a digital platform and then built a sustained winning business model around it (e.g., Netflix)—your digital evolution will need to follow this road map.

Building the Five-Stage Model Further into Disciplines

Digital Transformation 5.0 provides a road map to help set the correct end state and assess where you are in that journey. How successfully you move along that journey is driven by discipline. Our road map will be complemented with tangible disciplines and eventually checklists to bring the right level of rigor for successful digital transformation. For that, we need lessons from the aircraft industry, and some Swiss cheese. (Yes, really!)

Learning from the Disciplines of Aircraft Takeoff

The fact that airplanes have high safety standards isn't a surprise. The bigger surprise should be that takeoffs have become highly automated and reliable *despite being highly complex endeavors.* In today's world, several coincidental failures need to occur for aircrafts to fail during takeoff. Aircraft manufacturers use the principle of layered security, also known as the Swiss cheese model (see sidebar), to understand and mitigate the risk of a failure.

What Does Aviation Safety Have to Do with Swiss Cheese?

The Swiss cheese model of accident causation states that human systems are similar to slices of Swiss cheese that are placed vertically in front of each other. The holes in the cheese represent defects or weaknesses in each system and tend to be of different sizes and positions. If a line can pass through the stack of cheese holes, then that represents failure of the system as a whole, leading to an accident. The goal in designing the system is to reduce the probability of an accident by making improvements on both "holes" and "number of slices."

James Reason, who created the Swiss cheese model, believed that accidents can happen for four reasons: organizational influences, unsafe supervision, preconditions for unsafe acts, and the unsafe acts themselves. The Swiss cheese model has been applied extensively to reduce accident management in both the aviation and medical industries.

To improve digital transformation reliability, I follow a similar approach. The top two causes of failure in moving from one stage to the next have been identified. A checklist of questions helps determine whether each of these has been sufficiently addressed.

Flight safety in the early days of aviation was not a given. The airplanes—which were made of fabric, glue, and wood for the most part—made flying more a game of skill than process. Takeoff and landing crashes were common. The intervening decades have seen an improvement in both design and methodology. The Swiss cheese model was one of the risk-minimization techniques employed. Once the drivers of failure were understood, it became possible to redesign technical products, processes, systems, and people capabilities to minimize or eliminate them. (The airline checklists are simply mechanisms to follow rigorous processes for items that cannot be fully automated or eliminated.)

My work at P&G's GBS proved that understanding the drivers of digital transformation failure from one stage to the next, and then counteracting those failures with checklists, could be applied to digital transformation success as well. I have identified and confirmed very specific reliability drivers (and therefore disciplines) to improve the success rate of each of the five stages of digital transformation.

> There are very specific reliability drivers (and therefore checklists) to improve the success rate of each of the five stages of digital transformation.

The Surprising Disciplines of How to Take Off and Stay Ahead

Figure 3 illustrates the two risk factors (and therefore checklist items) per stage in our five-stage model.

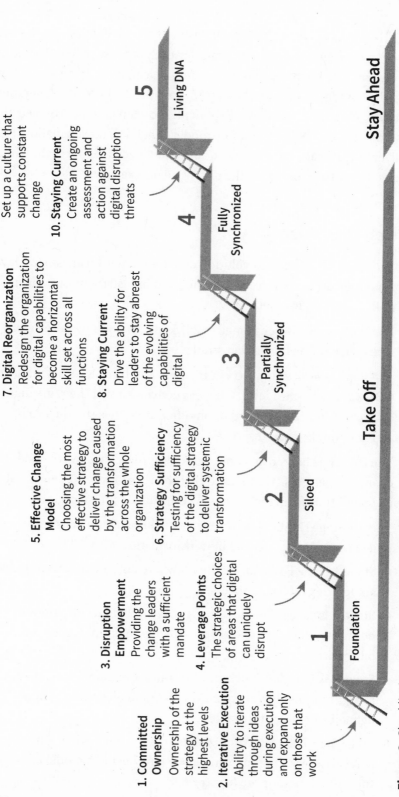

Figure 3 Checklist items to move up the five stages

The next part of the book will flesh out the five stages and the two respective discipline areas necessary for each of these to be successful.

After that, I will share how all these disciplines can be assembled together by describing in chapter 13 how the P&G Next Generation Services execution unfolded. Exponential organizations provided the inspiration. The NGS operating model (Digital Transformation 5.0) delivered the road map for execution. The checklist approach, which evolved over time, provided the discipline for execution.

Chapter Summary

- The Fourth Industrial Revolution demands a new business strategy from the current one created in the third industrial era (i.e., the rise of PCs and the internet).

- P&G's GBS saw this challenge in 2015 and set about creating a proactive digital transformation strategy.

- The shared services industry at the time had three levels of maturity. GBS was at the third level. GBS was convinced that the same digital disruption forces that acted upon other industries should also be acting upon the shared services industry.

- The issue was how to go about this disruptive change with good chances of success. We realized that the reason why 70 percent of all digital transformations failed was insufficient discipline.

- The five stage Digital Transformation 5.0 model provides a disciplined road map to succeed in transformation.

  ▸ **Stage 1** is the Foundation. This is where enterprises are actively automating internal processes.

  ▸ **Stage 2** is called Siloed. You might see individual functions or businesses start to use disruptive technologies to create new business models.

  ▸ **Stage 3** is Partially Synchronized transformation. The CEO has recognized the disruptive power of digital technologies and defined a digital future state.

  ▸ **Stage 4**, or Fully Synchronized, marks the point where an enterprise-wide digital platform or new business model has fully taken root for the first time.

- ▶ **Stage 5**, or Living DNA, is the step where the transformation becomes perpetual.

- Airplane safety has become a byword in reliable operations by understanding and eliminating risks in a disciplined manner. Frameworks like the Swiss cheese model, combined with operational discipline using checklists, are proven models.

- To move up reliably through the five stages of digital transformation, I have identified two disciplines to be checked for each.

Your Disciplines Checklist

Evaluate your digital transformation against the questions in figure 4 to follow a disciplined approach to each step in Digital Transformation 5.0.

Goal Setting	Foundation (Stage 1)	Siloed (Stage 2)	Partly Sync. (Stage 3)	Fully Sync. (Stage 4)	Living DNA (Stage 5)

1. Does the proposed transformation use two or more of the following— exponential technologies, outcome-based models, and exponential ecosystems?

2. Is the goal of your transformation to reinvent, as opposed to create incremental evolution?

3. Is the goal to deliver one or more of the following—new business model transformation, new technology-enabled product adjacency, or 10X operating efficiencies?

4. Is the intent of the transformation to drive a perpetual culture of transformation?

5. Is the proposed transformation enterprise wide, based on a formal strategy and driven from the top?

Figure 4 Your disciplines checklist for goal setting

Part II

The Five Stages of Digital Transformation

Stage 1

Foundation

What Is Stage 1?	Automation (or digitalization) of processes. It delivers enterprise value by using technology to do work more efficiently and builds the foundation for further transformation.
Causes of Failure	Teams lose sight of the intended business value being targeted, or they execute poorly.
Disciplines to Address Risks	▪ *Committed ownership* of the strategy at the highest levels. ▪ *Iterative execution* to avoid major implementation failures.

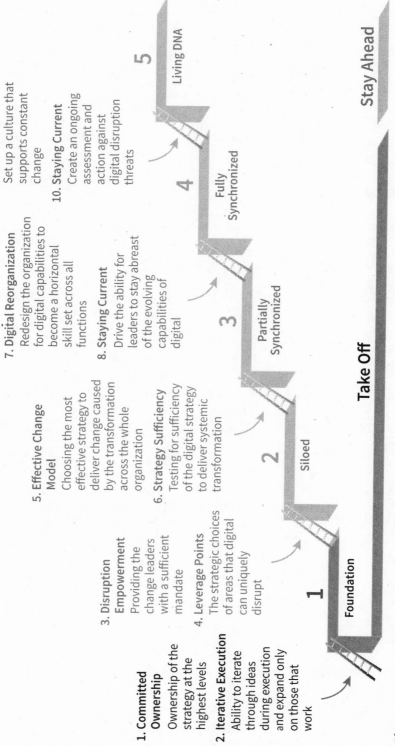

1. Committed Ownership
Ownership of the strategy at the highest levels

2. Iterative Execution
Ability to iterate through ideas during execution and expand only on those that work

3. Disruption Empowerment
Providing the change leaders with a sufficient mandate

4. Leverage Points
The strategic choices of areas that digital can uniquely disrupt

5. Effective Change Model
Choosing the most effective strategy to deliver change caused by the transformation across the whole organization

6. Strategy Sufficiency
Testing for sufficiency of the digital strategy to deliver systemic transformation

7. Digital Reorganization
Redesign the organization for digital capabilities to become a horizontal skill set across all functions

8. Staying Current
Drive the ability for leaders to stay abreast of the evolving capabilities of digital

9. Agile Culture
Set up a culture that supports constant change

10. Staying Current
Create an ongoing assessment and action against digital disruption threats

1 Foundation
2 Siloed
3 Partially Synchronized
4 Fully Synchronized
5 Living DNA

Take Off

Stay Ahead

Figure 5 Stage 1 digital transformation disciplines

Chapter 3

Committed Ownership

My family and I lived in Singapore in 1998 and again in 2012. The settling-in experience in 1998 was particularly striking. We were quite literally settled in within three to four days of moving into the country. Our personal goods had been delivered and unpacked; bank accounts set up; utilities, TV, internet, and phone connections activated; and driver's licenses converted. Our experience with the bureaucracy in the country was amazing.

Keep in mind that this was in 1998, when most things were not done online. In Singapore, the push to digitize was already evident at that time. For instance, hardly anyone seemed to use checks for banking. Routine payments were accomplished with direct transfers between bank accounts using a local system called GIRO (General Interbank Recurring Order).

Today, Singapore is ranked number one in the world in a digitization index called the Networked Readiness Index (NRI) by the World Economic Forum. It measures how well an economy is using information and communications technologies to boost competitiveness and well-being. Singapore is followed by Finland, Sweden, and Norway. The US ranks number five. The questions we need to ask are: How did Singapore get to this position? Who owns the strategy for digital? And what role does the leadership play?

Singapore is a good case study in successfully moving up the five stages of digital transformation. It has demonstrated high success rates in the basic automation efforts of Stage 1 transformation, and it continues to be a model for public sector enterprises to stay ahead via perpetual Stage 5 transformation. It demonstrates most of the disciplines of how to take off and stay ahead on digital transformation. In particular, what struck me in 1998 was the committed ownership of Prime Minister Lee Kuan Yew and his government on the strategy of using digital technology as a transformative engine. Most governments at the time made noises about using digital technologies, but the Singapore leadership was truly committed.

Why Digital Transformation Needs Special Commitment and Ownership from Leaders

One of the first lessons I learned as a leader was to never outsource a problem. This isn't a radical insight by itself. Management gurus from decades ago preached that you can delegate responsibility but not accountability. And yet, in my analysis of digital transformation failures, it was surprising to see how many of them could trace their roots back to leaders over-delegating their digital transformations.

Digital technologies are new and fast evolving, which means there's a need for special attention from sponsors of digital transformation.

Much of this tends to be due to well-intentioned empowerment of their people. That's noble, except for one thing—over-delegation isn't empowerment; it's delegation of complexity.

Here's the issue relative to digital transformation. Digital technologies are new and fast evolving, which means there's a need for special attention from leaders. Driving clarity of the business issue, providing personal commitment to spend time connecting the business issue to digital transformation strategies, and ongoing barrier busting during transformation—all these roles cannot be delegated. That's true in the case of a Stage 1 automation project and even more true of high-stakes Stage 5 transformations. The level of sponsors in the organization is driven by the size of transformation; it could be entry-level managers for tiny automation projects or a business owner or prime minister for true Stage 5 transformation. Regardless, even for the basic Stage 1 transformation, sponsors cannot over-delegate digital transformation without serious risks of failure.

The Leader's Critical Role in Digital Transformations

In a *Harvard Business Review* article, "Digital Leadership Is Not an Optional Part of Being a CEO,"[17] Josh Bersin makes the case that the

CEO needs to lead the digital charge for their company by having the company "act digital," not just "do digital." His research into what he calls "digital DNA" identified twenty-three new management practices, including empowerment, experimentation, collaboration, data, and speed. In other words, the role of the CEO is not just to sponsor the digital effort, appoint a chief digital officer, hire executives from Silicon Valley, bring in consultants, and provide funding and rah-rah leadership. The CEO also needs to create the right conditions of a true digital enterprise—demonstrating personal skin in the game on the goals, being hands-on in translating the goals into digital transformation strategies, and constantly breaking barriers in execution. This role of committed ownership of digital transformation may start at the early stages of digital transformation, but it becomes nonnegotiable at Stage 3 (Partially Synchronized) and beyond, where there is a need for enterprise-wide change. The consistent success of Singapore in driving digital transformation amply demonstrates the effect of leadership commitment to the process.

Singapore Leadership's Committed Ownership of Its Digital Transformation Goals

Singapore's current prime minister, Lee Hsien Loong, is a computer science and math graduate and has the advantage of an in-depth understanding of the power of digital technologies. More important is how he, along with his government leaders, plays a highly visible role in leading the digitization efforts. He has shared on Facebook the code for C++ programs that he wrote to solve Sudoku puzzles. He initiated Singapore's "Smart Nation" digitization strategy and runs all the digitization programs out of the prime minister's office (i.e., the highest level of government in the country).

This commitment isn't a recent phenomenon, though. Singapore's journey with digital government started in the 1980s. Under the leadership of the country's first prime minister, Lee Kuan Yew, the government decided to differentiate itself through information and communications technology (ICT). Given the strength of this personal ownership and consistent commitment, Singapore's results in digitization are perhaps not surprising.

Singapore's Digital Journey

Singapore's number one ranking on the World Economic Forum's digitization index is the result of consistent leadership commitment over almost four decades. It started with the decision to computerize the civil service in 1981. The Civil Service Computerization Programme (CSCP) was aimed at manpower savings, operational efficiency improvement, better information support for decision making, and certain pioneer services for the public. This modest start has mushroomed over time to become a highly ambitious strategy. Singapore aims to be a leading provider of digital services for citizens as well as industry, driving a competitive advantage vs. other countries.

In May 2017, the Singapore government announced the creation of the Smart Nation and Digital Government Group (SNDGG), directly under the prime minister's office. The types of capabilities targeted are broad. In urban mobility, this ranges from using data analytics to better run public transportation to the implementation of self-driving vehicles. Under the Smart Nation program, Singapore plans to improve quality of life, create economic opportunity, and build a closer community.

Digitization Outcomes

The results have been remarkable. The efficiency of services provided to its citizens, residents, and businesses is outstanding. The customer satisfaction rating for its government eServices is well above 90 percent—a rare phenomenon for any country.

Here are a few examples of why the eServices program has such an excellent reputation. The Singapore eCitizen portal provides one-stop-shop access to all the information and eServices a citizen needs. SingPass is a single-authentication password to transact with all government agencies online, whether filing tax returns, applying for a passport, or registering a company. Singapore's Online Business Licensing Service (OBLS) is a one-stop portal to apply for all the required government licenses in a single online transaction. Most startups get all their licenses without having to visit a government counter. Not surprisingly, Singapore was ranked first in the "ease of doing business" index by the World Bank. Singapore offers about 1,600 online services and more than 300 mobile services to its citizens and businesses. Its relentless quest for digital excellence pushes its citizens and businesses to innovate and adopt new technology, giving the country an edge in efficiency over its peers.

The Sponsor's Role on Goal Translation and Barrier Busting in Transformations

A deeper dive into the specific role played by Singapore's leaders, among other successful sponsors of digital transformation, uncovers two sets of activities—clearly translating the business issue into digital transformation strategy elements, and barrier busting. Both are not one-time activities; rather, they are ongoing.

The goal-setting and translation role has been mentioned earlier in the chapter, where I discuss Josh Bersin's *Harvard Business Review* article, "Digital Leadership Is Not an Optional Part of Being a CEO."[18] The nonoptional elements that Bersin lists include many cultural and organizational factors. The specific translation of the enterprise's business goals into these factors—both one-time and ongoing—must be led at the top (i.e., CEO, business owner, government leader, etc.).

The specific translation of the enterprise's business goals into digital transformation strategies—both one-time and ongoing—must be led at the top (i.e., CEO, business owner, government leader, etc.).

Less understood but equally important is the role of the leader in barrier busting during the transformation itself. It's a pity that this is usually not emphasized, because this is where a majority of transformations fail. The more complex the change (regardless of transformation stage level), the stronger the need for this ongoing barrier busting. Not surprisingly, Stage 5 transformation needs the most help because it has the highest stakes and involves the most complex changes. P&G's historical success in driving brilliant standardization and scale in its financial, sales, and supply chain systems is a testimony to this. It's a perfect example of driving highly complex Stage 1 transformation and relying on strong, committed ownership from its leaders to deliver it. That project is unrelated to our main NGS story, but it illustrates the key role of sponsors for barrier busting.

How P&G Maintains a Best-In-Class Enterprise Resource Planning System

P&G is one of a handful of large global companies that has a single standard enterprise resource planning (ERP) system for all its global operations. This is essentially a standard digital backbone of financial, order processing, distribution, and manufacturing platforms across more than one hundred countries. This enables enterprise-wide planning and execution of financial and physical operations across the world. ERP systems are the backbone of most companies, and P&G uses SAP for this.

In terms of automation, getting to one ERP system across the world is the holy grail of most global companies. It is a Stage 1 transformation. P&G got there in the early 2000s and, more importantly, continues to maintain it despite continued acquisitions that involve integrating new ERP systems from the acquired companies. Standardizing on one ERP is extremely difficult, and keeping it as one, despite acquisitions and restructures, is even harder. The larger and more complex the organization, the more difficult the transformation.

What has enabled P&G to get there is committed ownership from leadership. The business goal is clear—enable global scale by using one ERP system. More interesting is the role of leadership literally every year in barrier busting on the multiple ERP-related projects that are generated by acquisitions, legal and tax changes, and the like.

Here's how this has happened. The major corporate ERP transformations are sponsored by the finance, supply chain, sales, and global business services presidents. Although GBS typically leads the transformation, there is full ownership of the goals and true hands-on engagement on execution from these function-leader sponsors and the individual business unit presidents.

When P&G acquired the $10 billion-plus Gillette company in 2005, I moved up to the Gillette headquarters in Boston as interim chief information officer. Gillette had an enviable ERP solution also based on SAP, which had been tailored for their shaving and battery businesses. Inevitably, there were issues related to where the Gillette work processes and systems would need to change to fit the P&G standards and where P&G standards could adopt Gillette's. The number of escalated issues ran into the hundreds.

However, as usual at P&G, there was almost a magical cadence that the ERP execution team and sponsors fell into. The C-suite sponsors were involved personally on a daily and weekly basis. The decisions ranged from whether to change the date of a certain systems cut-over to keep away from the busy Christmas business season to redesigning corporate measures of financial reporting. The work of the execution teams was hard, but without the active barrier busting from the sponsors, we could never have achieved success, including becoming an industry success story. This happens routinely at P&G, thus enabling robust sustenance of the globally standard ERP process.

Why Don't We See More Committed Ownership from Leaders?

If committed ownership can deliver such powerful results, then why don't we see more of it? There are several factors at play, but the one that needs to be addressed most urgently is, frankly, digital literacy of leadership. Traditional organizations whose base business is not rooted in digital technology are highly vulnerable here.

The Digital Literacy Challenge at the Leadership Level

The personal challenge of digital literacy for many senior executives, including CEOs in the public or private sector, is daunting. Running a digitally enabled operation requires an appreciation of IT technology that goes well beyond day-to-day use of IT tools. Not every leader can be a C++ programmer in the mold of Prime Minister Lee Hsien Loong, but there is a need to quickly come up to speed on the *possibilities* of technology at a minimum. For instance, understanding what artificial intelligence, software robots, or platform solutions can do for your business is required, at minimum, in order to lead an exercise into the art of the possible.

The IT industry, which tends to hype technologies, hasn't helped on this issue. For many executives, this leads to an overreliance on their chief information officers and chief digital officers for digital strategy. The problem with this is that digital disruption strategy (creating new business models for the overall business) is different from corporate IT strategy (driving automation and productivity in daily operations). According to a recent study, 68 percent of technology spending is now coming from budgets outside of IT. Delegating the creation of new disruptive business models to the CIO or CDO will never be as good as turning every leader in your organization into a passable digital leader. Every business function leader and every business unit leader needs to make and own the choices about how they will digitize their part of the enterprise.

The Digital Literacy Challenge at the Board Level

Unfortunately, the lack of digital literacy becomes more pronounced higher up the chain. Ultimately, the board of directors is accountable for understanding digital trends and guiding the company appropriately. The top five largest companies in the world have great presence of what is starting to be known as "digital directors." They included leaders such as Microsoft cofounder Bill Gates, Intel chairman Andy Bryant, former Qwest Communications CEO Ed Mueller, former Yahoo president Susan Decker, former Yahoo CEO Marissa Mayer, Xerox CEO Ursula Burns, former IBM chairman Sam Palmisano, Instagram cofounder Kevin Systrom, and Comcast executive vice president Steve Burke. However, this isn't the norm. The consulting firm McKinsey & Company estimates that less than 20 percent of corporate boards have the digital literacy required for today's world and that less than 5 percent of the companies in North America have a technology committee. Many boards are therefore thoroughly underprepared given that existential threats can come from adjacent industries. The traditional style of operation that made board members successful may be exactly the thing that kills the company.

Digital literacy at the leadership levels is a huge issue, starting at the board level. Less than 20 percent of board members have the digital literacy required for today's world.

Nominating committees for boards must react quickly. In addition, board members need to get up to speed rapidly. As with the need for digital literacy at the leadership level, the board needs to understand the possibilities of digital technologies. Board members must spend a larger percentage of their time on digital strategy beyond the defensive cyber-security agendas. This level of digital sponsorship is not just appropriate; it is the distinguishing factor between companies that thrive in the Fourth Industrial Revolution and those that get left behind.

■　■　■

There's no substitute for committed digital transformation ownership at the highest levels in any organization. The fast pace of change on digital technologies makes this a unique challenge for traditional enterprises. Learning from technical experts inside and outside the organization is a valid approach, but delegating strategy and barrier busting is dangerous. The best leaders of digital transformation bring in three unique elements—sufficient knowledge, their time, and their skills to break barriers on digital transformations.

Chapter Summary

- Digital is a relatively new and fast-changing area. It requires special engagement at the leadership level.

- In Singapore, which is ranked the most digital nation in the world, Prime Minister Lee Hsien Loong has the set the tone for their digital program by communicating his personal commitment. Singapore's digital program is also run out of the prime minister's office.

- Translating business goals into digital strategy is a key role that leaders cannot delegate. This becomes even more important at higher stages of digital transformation.

- A more important role of a leader is barrier busting during execution of digital transformations. P&G's success in getting to one standard ERP system across the world is a case study in supporting digital transformations by quickly removing barriers in execution.

- For this level of ownership at the top to be true, there is an implied level of digital literacy required of all leaders, starting with the executive leadership and the board of directors. Unfortunately, this is still a challenge in most cases.

Your Disciplines Checklist

Evaluate your digital transformation against the questions in figure 6 to follow a disciplined approach to each step in Digital Transformation 5.0.

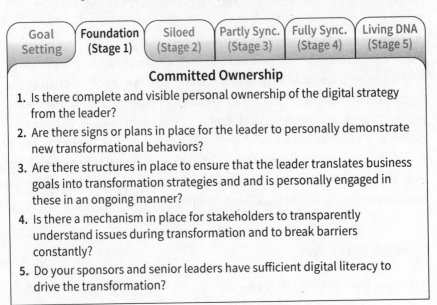

| Goal Setting | Foundation (Stage 1) | Siloed (Stage 2) | Partly Sync. (Stage 3) | Fully Sync. (Stage 4) | Living DNA (Stage 5) |

Committed Ownership

1. Is there complete and visible personal ownership of the digital strategy from the leader?
2. Are there signs or plans in place for the leader to personally demonstrate new transformational behaviors?
3. Are there structures in place to ensure that the leader translates business goals into transformation strategies and and is personally engaged in these in an ongoing manner?
4. Is there a mechanism in place for stakeholders to transparently understand issues during transformation and to break barriers constantly?
5. Do your sponsors and senior leaders have sufficient digital literacy to drive the transformation?

Figure 6 Your disciplines checklist for committed ownership.

Chapter 4

Iterative Execution

It was midnight on Tuesday, October 1, 2013. This was D-day for the team leading the project on the federal web portal for the Affordable Care Act (ACA), HealthCare.gov, more popularly called the Obamacare exchange. As the website opened for business, watched by teams from the Centers for Medicare and Medicaid Services and their contractors, the initial reactions were somewhat positive. The traffic on the exchange was higher than expected, but that was good news for a White House that had worried about hitting enrollment numbers.

However, at the offices of CGI Federal, one of the main contractors that built the site, the mood was decidedly darker. IT technicians were realizing that the software running the exchange was starting to crumble as customers faced delays in creating accounts. Shortly after that, the website crashed. This was an inauspicious start to the HealthCare. gov launch for President Barack Obama, whose signature legislative accomplishment would eventually become successful, but was tarnished slightly by a substandard technology project.

The reality is that the Obamacare website issue was more a discipline failure than a technology failure. Unfortunately, it's a simple tale of an IT project gone terribly wrong that's all too common in organizations. Though the HealthCare.gov project was big and complex, there's no reason why it could not have been developed iteratively, thus breaking up the risk of a big-bang start into many smaller deliveries. In IT software development, this technique is called agile software development, and although it was used in parts for the ACA portal development, the predominant mode of delivery was a big-bang technique known as "waterfall," where long durations of design and development are followed by the big launch.

When it comes to digital transformation executions, however, the bigger they are the harder they fall. De-risking a digital transformation, whether Stage 1 or higher, by chunking the work into smaller iterative deliveries while constantly learning is a key tenet for avoiding big, embarrassing failures. Unsurprisingly, these principles are applicable beyond software development. Lean startup, the methodology drawing attention from large and small enterprises to shorten product development cycles and accelerate determining if a business model is viable, is based on the same principle. The goal is to use several small experiments based on hypothesis testing to validate learning before iteratively launching products.

De-risking a digital transformation, whether Stage 1 or higher, by chunking the work into smaller iterative deliveries and constant learning is a key tenet for avoiding big, embarrassing failures.

Amazon.com's first website, which launched in July 1995, had none of the slick designs, intelligent algorithms, or indeed any of its current capabilities at all beyond perusing a catalog of books and placing an order. Their internal operations were equally basic, with employees manually procuring books, packing them up, and driving them to the post office. However, this afforded Amazon the opportunity to leverage what worked and discard what did not, inexorably moving toward its founder Jeff Bezos's vision of one day becoming "an everything store."

How to Apply Iterative Execution to Complex, Multi-Project Programs

The HealthCare.gov website hiccup provides excellent lessons on avoiding a big-bang failure using iterative execution beyond individual project levels. How do you apply this to complex, multi-project programs like an entire organization's transformation?

The principle of breaking up a large risky effort into smaller iterative chunks still holds. You can think big without betting the farm on one idea.

Transforming an entire enterprise will take more than one project; it takes a portfolio of projects. In this situation the strategy of de-risking execution is as simple as creating a portfolio of projects that include some big bets and other sure bets so that the total portfolio is sufficient to deliver the overall targeted goal. This was the lesson that the Denver International Airport program learned very painfully thirty years ago.

Why Did the Initial Healthcare.gov Launch Run Into Issues?

The ACA portal project issue, while embarrassing, was hardly unique. In fact, it's a great case study precisely because it is like so many other transformation failures.

As background, the Patient Protection and Affordable Care Act, or Affordable Care Act (ACA), or more commonly Obamacare, was meant to be President Barack Obama's signature legislative accomplishment. It was signed into law on March 23, 2010, to provide a breakthrough in reducing the number of uninsured citizens in the US. The portal HealthCare.gov was planned to go online a little over three years later, on October 1, 2013. Shortly after midnight, a couple of thousand users signed on to start the process to enroll for health care. The website promptly crashed. It was initially thought that the bottleneck was in the traffic for logging on to the website. However, once that was resolved, other issues showed up. It would be months before the technical issues were resolved. When the dust settled and the open enrollment period officially ended on April 15, 2014, an estimated 13.5 million people had applied for coverage and about 8 million selected a coverage plan. Though that number was above target, indicating success for the health-care policy itself, the website issues were unfortunately embarrassing.

In my opinion, there were three major causes for this. I believe it could have been avoided by using the two disciplines in this section: committed ownership and iterative execution. Here were the three root causes of the rocky HealthCare.gov launch:

1. The bigger they are the harder they fall. The HealthCare.gov IT project was a monster. According to Forbes magazine, there were fifty-five contractors, five federal agencies, thirty-six states, three hundred private-sector insurers, and over four thousand insurance plans involved. A typical user was expected to work through seventy-five screens, and in total over a thousand screens were designed. The large scale of HealthCare.gov was unavoidable. And most large organizations that pursue a big disruptive idea will likely involve a big scope. The question is: How do you transform the monster into bite-size chunks?

The HealthCare.gov website was developed partly by using iterative software development methodologies like agile. However, the issue is that most of the in-market user experience came only at the end, when the website was formally opened for business. This is where methodologies like lean startup come in. These force a discipline to get real-life in-market user experience every few weeks. Waiting until the end of the project to discover that your product doesn't work when assembled is highly unpleasant.

2. Who's in charge? The HealthCare.gov experience provides great lessons in assigning accountability. Kathleen Sebelius, the Health and Human Services (HHS) secretary, was the direct link to President Obama on this project. She appointed a chief information officer to manage her IT projects. In a memo published in August 2011, the White House Office of Management and Budget strongly recommended that the CIO should take accountability for all IT projects. In reality, the HHS CIO was never in charge.

It was the Centers for Medicare and Medicaid Services (CMS) that ran the project. Further, CMS decided to in-source the systems integration (the responsibility to manage various development partners as well as technically piece together all their solutions). The only issue was that CMS had insufficient capability to be the systems integrator. To make things worse, there was considerable infighting within CMS on both the user experience as well as technical operation of the website. As a result, the contractors didn't receive the guidance they needed. Nothing slows down a project more effectively than fuzzy accountability.

3. Iterative customer feedback. Perhaps the most important lesson for digital transformation is the need for iteration with the customer. Amazon.com's first website looked terrible but enabled the company to collect user feedback. Unfortunately for Healthcare.gov, most other considerations—policy, cost, political commitments—overrode the goal of iterating with users. Deconstructing large transformational efforts into many small user-noticeable units is critical.

Once the issues became public, the right project leadership was quickly established. Experts from Silicon Valley brought in the right iterative executional disciplines, and the issues disappeared.

The good news for digital transformations is that they don't need be executed as big-bang monsters. Iterative delivery processes like agile and lean startup can effectively deliver the most complex transformations with much lower risk.

Why the Futuristic Denver Airport Baggage System Project Failed

In 1989, the city of Denver started work to build a bold new state-of-the-art airport. It was meant to be the largest airport in the US and a major hub for airline transportation, doubling its capacity to process fifty million passengers annually. Aircraft turnaround time, which is the duration between when a plane lands to when it takes off again, was envisioned to be cut to thirty minutes. For contrast, regular airlines even today take forty to sixty minutes for short-haul flight turnaround and multiple hours for long-haul. Faster turnaround time means a bigger competitive advantage in the airport business.

To drive this level of efficiency, a new, highly automated baggage-handling system was envisioned. The idea was futuristic. At check-in the agent would attach a glue-backed label to the bag. A fully automated conveyor belt would then take over. All baggage movement between check-in, transfer, aircraft loading, and pick-up would be automatic. This was an excellent example of a technology-driven disruption that could lead to competitive advantage.

What it actually led to was a delay of sixteen months in opening the new airport and cost overruns worth $560 million.[19] Even after that delay, instead of connecting three concourses, the system supported one concourse, and even then, only for outbound flights. And in that small execution, the baggage system still tore up and lost bags. In 2005, the only airline left on the system finally pulled the plug. And it gave the world another great example of an ambitious transformation gone horribly wrong. What the Denver airport envisioned was the future;[20] what it got was a Godzilla of a system that happily chewed luggage and even at its best speed would not match human baggage-handler timings.

> **Executions of entirely new systems and capabilities must be based on a portfolio-effect assumption—that some parts of the high-risk portfolio will be successful and others will fail.**

The lesson to be learned from Denver's system is that when it comes to digital transformations, vision and hope are not strategies. Executions of breakthrough new systems and capabilities must be based on a portfolio-effect assumption—that some parts of the high-risk portfolio will be successful and others will fail. Higher risk, big-bet digital transformations need to be based on portfolio-sufficiency plans, not very different from what financial wealth planners do. The portfolio in total must be sufficient to deliver the outcome.

An Iterative Execution Approach to Digital Transformation

Iterative execution for large-scale digital transformation is designed to address issues such as those of the HealthCare.gov and Denver International Airport baggage system rollouts. It blends the principles of breaking up waterfall methods into smaller iterative pieces for each project and creating a portfolio of different projects of different levels of risk/return.

At P&G's Next Generation Services, we applied this mash-up successfully. We applied fast two-week iterations to individual experiments (projects) and subprojects and created a portfolio mix to ensure sufficiency of the entire transformation program. This broke up the "one big bet" approach to digital transformation into smaller lower-risk projects by running a portfolio of initiatives.

> **Successful transformations blend smaller iterative execution for each project and a portfolio of different projects. Each project has a different level of risk/return.**

Figure 7 depicts the approach that was used at NGS. The overall NGS business opportunity (#1 in the figure) was to deliver very specific cost savings, top-line improvement, and user-experience improvement. The disruptive idea (#2) was to create the NGS ecosystem and operate it as an industry disruption forum. The portfolio of experiments (projects) (#3) was a collection of very specific disruptive needs

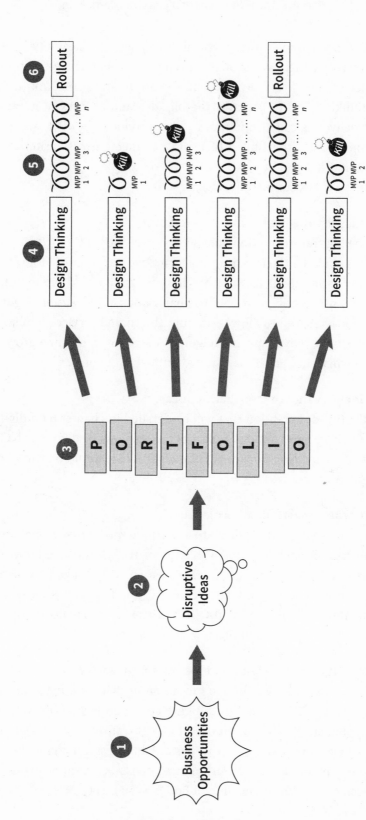

Figure 7 Combining iterative execution and a portfolio of projects

of P&G's GBS that additionally had industry-wide replicability so the development partners we brought in could commercialize the products outside P&G. Every project followed an iterative execution using design thinking (#4) to generate the big idea and a series of iterative product deliveries called minimum viable products (MVPs) (#5), and each project was either killed (if it did not meet success criteria) or rolled out if it did (#6).

Here is a quick summary of the six steps:

Step 1: Identify the big business opportunity.

This is the big transformation goal-setting exercise for the overall program. This could be the massive transformative purpose (MTP), which is a highly aspirational tagline that has the ability to drive extreme motivation, as described in Salim Ismail's book *Exponential Organizations*. For NGS, the MTP was "disrupt the shared services industry." The goal was to deliver specific ongoing cost savings, top-line growth, and user-experience gains that were identified at the outset.

Step 2: Identify the transformation ideas.

This is the big idea creation that will be detailed in chapter 6 on digital leverage points. This happens as part of the business strategy. For NGS, this was to create an exponential organization that would be run as an industry ecosystem.

Step 3: Create a portfolio of projects.

Break up the big disruptive idea into a portfolio mix of many small iterative projects. In NGS, we used a strategy of 10-5-4-1, where for every ten experiments (projects) undertaken, we could kill five, and of the remaining ones, four might turn out to be 2X or 4X types of ideas, but the remaining one would be a 10X. This process allows many small-bet projects to fail in the pursuit of a few big home runs.

Step 4: Use iterative design processes to design each project.

At NGS, we used design thinking to come up with the big transformation project ideas. A design thinking approach is superior to process mapping approaches when used for 10X transformations. Design thinking helps focus only on the desired business outcome (e.g., a room to stay in, in the case of Airbnb) and does not presuppose historical processes (e.g., the ownership of hotels as an asset).

Step 5: Use iterative execution methodology
such as lean startup or agile.

Iterative execution approaches force you to break the idea into customer-focused building blocks and then build and field-test minimum viable product (MVP) executions. This facilitates building on the MVP building blocks until you have built out the big idea fully. In the case of the Denver baggage system, the MVP could have been as simple as field-testing a small part of the vision first (e.g., electronic baggage tagging for one airline or one concourse).

Step 6: Roll out only the successful projects.

The advantage of the previous five steps in iterative execution is that it helps not just to pivot within a project but also to choose to use only the most successful projects among the portfolio.

This iterative execution approach has one other major benefit—it delivers speed, or "innovation velocity." Because you successfully chunk the big transformation into many small executions, the time, money, and risk involved in each small execution is significantly smaller. The ideas are therefore able to move along much faster. Speed is a very big enabler of success in transformation. Traditional thinking suggests that "better," "faster," and "cheaper" are together a zero-sum game, i.e., if you increase some, you reduce the others. My experience on digital transformation is that if you push for speed, you get "better" and "faster" as side effects.

The Importance of Speed and Acceleration in Digital Transformations

Speed of execution matters in digital transformation not just because digital transformation is an urgent issue but because speed generates enthusiasm, momentum, and the right mindset.

I'd like to offer the analogy of an airplane takeoff for digital transformation takeoff. In the case of airplanes taxiing for takeoff, acceleration, which is the rate of change of speed, is directly related to the distance rolled on the runway. The slower the acceleration, the longer the distance needed before the aircraft achieves takeoff speed. If the aircraft never achieves the required acceleration, it cannot take off on the given runway. That's not too dissimilar to digital transformations. Acceleration, or rather the lack of it, can become a challenge. The initial experiments take so long that both stakeholders and organizations never see momentum develop. The disruption never takes off.

This issue is compounded for Stage 4 and Stage 5 transformations aimed at surviving industrial revolutions. The rapid pace of change in technology means that each digital idea has a shorter-than-usual shelf life, which gives digital transformation much shorter runways to work with. Or in other words, digital transformations need higher acceleration rates during industrial revolutions.

Speed and iterative execution complement each other to dramatically reduce risk of failure of digital transformations.

I would recommend that organizations on the path to digital transformation adopt speed (or in particular "innovation velocity") as a key metric. Speed and iterative execution complement each other to dramatically reduce risk of failure.

Speed (Innovation Velocity) as a Metric

Innovation velocity—the pace of invention—is a key metric in many forward-thinking organizations. Given the shorter runway for digital transformations, evaluating a large funnel of ideas, each executed at low cost and high speed, is the best bet for hitting a few successes. This focus on speed is an even bigger challenge in larger, more stable organizations that aren't usually known for rapid or low-cost iterations. Successful tech companies like Amazon, Netflix, and Alphabet have built this expectation of fast iteration into their cultures. Start-ups, on the other hand, tend to work on one big idea but are excellent at low-cost and high-speed iterations. The motivation system in a start-up helps with agility. When the money runs out, the game is over, and you need to find a new job. This obviously doesn't quite work the same way in larger organizations, given their cultures of job security and stability. The answer is to set up a model for processing ideas rapidly and iteratively that works equally well in large organizations. Money will never be the same constraint in larger organizations as in start-ups. The alternative is to make time the big constraint instead.

Why More Organizations Don't Drive Speed (and What You Can Do about It)

Most leaders already know that speed is an important driver of success on digital transformation. I strongly believe that the reason most organizations are not able to drive transformation at speed is related to structural issues. There are two main reasons for this.

I call the first the "clock speed" issue. A "clock speed" of operation is the normal pace at which decisions and operational change happen at the organization. (I have borrowed the term from the computing industry, where clock speed is the operating speed of a computer.) Since digital transformation efforts require operating at higher speeds, they generate conflicts within the organization, but this can be overcome, as I'll discuss later. The second issue is the "two worlds" situation, wherein the core organization's normal operations conflict with the change driven by the transformation team who wants to change it. This could be in the form of policies, practices, or other conflicts related to changing the operations. Here are ways to address both issues.

An Approach to Address "Clock Speed" Issues

At the NGS team, we had set about creating a new model that would deliver high-speed, low-cost iterations in 2015. If time was to be made the design constraint, then our operating model would need to visibly measure and publicize innovation velocity. The operating model had the usual five stages involved in innovation—landscape assessment, design, hypothesis testing, field testing, and rollout. To bring the element of innovation velocity into it, each stage was assigned a time goal. NGS came up with a convenient exponential series in months that would be associated with each respective stage—1-2-4-8-16. The exponential series related to the maximum time available for each of the five stages of innovation. So, landscape assessment would be one month long, design stage would take two months, and so on.

To be fully transparent, this was a totally contrived and simplistic series of deadlines at first. However, as NGS gained more experience, these targets were fine-tuned for each project. So, for example, highly disruptive experiments (projects) could be assigned longer timing goals for field-testing and rollout than lesser transformational ones. Over time, the actual speed goals became less important than the sense of motivation that they created. Each project status was prominently displayed on an eighteen- by six-foot dashboard in real time, with a ticking clock showing results accomplished vs. time passed for the stage. The transparency via this dashboard of metrics generated more pride and self-motivation than any other reward system based on project outcomes alone.

Addressing "Two Worlds" Issues

The two-worlds issue occurs because most organizations become inherently slow due to checks and balances introduced over the years to manage risks. There are legal- and procurement-related boxes to be checked, IT policy and technology standards to be met, HR and labor relations compliance issues to be addressed, global work-process organizations to be aligned—the list goes on. To be clear, each of these steps has a purpose and value. The question is whether the full brunt of all these processes is necessary during the nascent stages of an idea or whether they can be applied iteratively and with increasing intensity over time as the transformation matures.

At NGS, we developed the idea of an innovation "firewall" to protect transformative ideas in the early stages of development. This wasn't a technical or physical firewall but a process firewall designed to shield disruptive innovation work from the normal brunt of corporate processes (except for mandatory ethics, security, and legal ones). Examples included the following:

- While normal vendor qualification might take weeks or months, any NGS vendor that met certain narrow criteria could be qualified within a day or two.

- Information security and risk qualification within certain boundaries (e.g., not involving proprietary or personal data) could be done in days vs. months.

- New technology architectures beyond those that were normally mandated standards could be used by NGS under specific conditions.

- HR processes were tailored for a high-agility environment (e.g., killing a nonperforming project was rewarded in NGS, whereas the overhead and personal risk of any project failure in the core organization would have been high).

Next, within the NGS team, we developed a set of reward systems that would encourage smart risk taking. A certain amount of intelligent failure for learning was allowed. I mentioned the 10-5-4-1 model earlier that allowed several project failures, some medium disruptions, and a few 10X disruptions. This was fine as long as the portfolio effect of all of them was still hugely transformational. Between the innovation firewall and the 10-5-4-1 risk system, the team felt comfortable to think big.

Chapter Summary

- The initial HealthCare.gov website hiccup provides an important lesson on breaking up large "waterfall" projects into smaller iterative executions.

- When dealing with large transformations that include several high-risk projects, it is important to have a project portfolio mix that combines some high-risk ventures with other lower-risk ventures to ensure that the total mix delivers sufficient transformation.

- NGS created a six-step iterative execution approach to de-risk the digital disruption strategy by breaking it up into a portfolio mix of many projects and then using iterative execution within individual projects.

- Speed of transformation (innovation velocity) is a great complementary part of iterative execution. Transformational projects executed at high speed and low(er) risk/cost have a better chance at success.

- Most organizations recognize the need for speed of transformation. They are unable to act upon it for two reasons—"clock speed" and "two worlds" issues.

- At NGS, the clock-speed issue was addressed by assigning each stage of the transformation project a limited time to complete.

- The two-worlds issue was addressed by creating a "firewall" that insulated the early innovations from the full brunt of normal organizational processes.

Your Disciplines Checklist

Evaluate your digital transformation against the questions in figure 8 to follow a disciplined approach to each step in Digital Transformation 5.0.

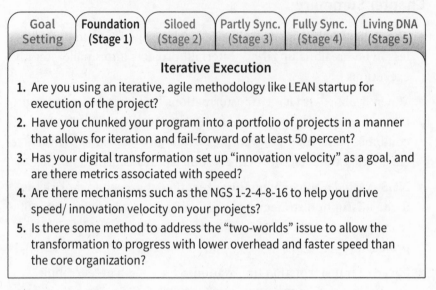

Goal Setting	Foundation (Stage 1)	Siloed (Stage 2)	Partly Sync. (Stage 3)	Fully Sync. (Stage 4)	Living DNA (Stage 5)

Iterative Execution

1. Are you using an iterative, agile methodology like LEAN startup for execution of the project?
2. Have you chunked your program into a portfolio of projects in a manner that allows for iteration and fail-forward of at least 50 percent?
3. Has your digital transformation set up "innovation velocity" as a goal, and are there metrics associated with speed?
4. Are there mechanisms such as the NGS 1-2-4-8-16 to help you drive speed/ innovation velocity on your projects?
5. Is there some method to address the "two-worlds" issue to allow the transformation to progress with lower overhead and faster speed than the core organization?

Figure 8 Your disciplines checklist for iterative execution

Stage 2

Siloed

What Is Stage 2?	The organic development of major digitally based processes and products, but only in parts of the organization. Individual leaders have recognized the threat of digital disruption and started creating new digital business models. Siloed transformations are a microcosm of what will hopefully become higher stages of digital transformation.
Causes of Failure	Common mistakes include under-powering change leaders and making incorrect choices in what to transform.
Disciplines to Address Risks	▪ *Disruption empowerment* of the change leaders. ▪ *Digital leverage* points identification.

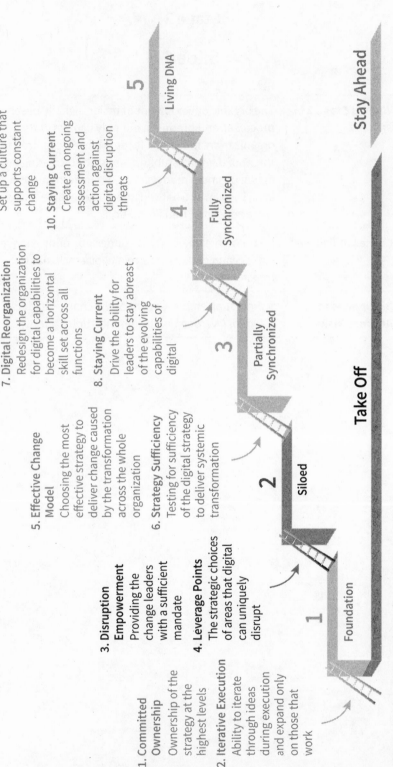

Figure 9 Stage 2 digital transformation disciplines

Chapter 5

Disruption Empowerment

Digital transformation is hard even at the Siloed level of Stage 2. It involves going against the grain of several things that have historically made the enterprise successful. The change is massive, and the change leaders will need an unprecedentedly broad mandate along with top-down and some bottom-up support. This is logical, and most leaders understand this. The challenge is in getting precise on what "support" means.

In this chapter, I develop the discipline of how to provide this support in more detail. This includes setting up an inspirational vision, or a massive transformative purpose (MTP), that rallies the entire organization. The second element is to provide very tangible "air cover" (i.e., support from higher up) for the change leaders to take the necessary risks. The third element is to create informal leadership motivation by announcing personal skin in the game for the change, and the final move is to overcome initial inertia by selecting a feeder pipeline of areas that can immediately show progress.

These four elements of support aren't random. They showed up as major factors for success in NGS and keep popping up in the case studies on why digital transformations fail. They are common to both digital transformation failures as well as nondigital. To illustrate this, I start with a couple of such examples. The first is the failed attempt to convert to the metric system in the United States.

Why the Effort to Introduce the Metric System in the United States Failed

Ever wonder why the US still hasn't adopted the metric system just like the rest of the world? It has not been for want of trying. There were several efforts, including those led by the National Bureau of Standards in the 1960s, an act from the US Congress in the late '60s, and even a law passed under the Metric Conversion Act of 1975 declaring the metric system the "preferred system of weights and measures for United States trade and commerce."

The failure of that last determined effort in the '70s and '80s is a good case study on the effect of fuzzy support from sponsors on major transformations. The execution almost immediately ran into indifference and resistance. In 1981, the United States Metric Board (USMB), which had been previously created to drive the transition to metric, reported to Congress that it would need a clear congressional mandate to accomplish its mission. They didn't get it. Finally, in 1982 the Reagan administration disbanded the USMB due to a combination of factors, including its lack of results as well as a push to cut government spending.

The fact that the USMB had to ask for a congressional mandate to lead the change is a clear sign that they were not empowered to execute the conversion. Contrast this outcome with the many successful digital transformations led by the Singapore government. It's a good lesson on the importance of empowering change.

Context for the Metric System Conversion Effort in the 1970s

The United States, Myanmar, and Liberia are the only three countries in the world that have not adopted or are in the process of adopting the metric system for weights and measures. To be fair, the US is more metric than it gets credit for. Even though you buy groceries by the pound, soft drinks are sold by the liter. Day-to-day popular usage (e.g., car speed in miles) continues with US customary units, but most of the scientific measurements in the US use the metric system. This disconnect is usually attributed to cost-benefit of a conversion effort: it would be very expensive to convert to the metric system, and the benefit is unclear to most people. The big chance to convert was in 1975. There was a plan, a law mandating it, and an official body to lead the transition. Except that the transformation failed.

The history of the effort to adopt the metric system goes all the way back to Thomas Jefferson. The first Congress meeting in 1789 took up the topic of weights and measures. Jefferson submitted a proposal for a decimal-based system that looked a lot like today's metric system. It was not adopted since it lacked support from the scientific community. Even Alexander Graham Bell is known to have made a plea in an address to the Committee on Coinage, Weights, and Measures of the US House of Representatives in 1906, saying, "Few people have any adequate conception of the amount of unnecessary labor involved in the use of our present weights and measures." That went nowhere to.

How the Effort to Implement the Metric System Failed

The best shot of conversion for the US came in the '60s and '70s. In 1964, the National Bureau of Standards (now called the National Institute of Standards and Technology, or NIST) moved the US closer to the metric system by declaring that it would adopt it except in areas of detrimental effect. With that, the pendulum seemed to swing in the direction of the metric system. In 1968, Congress chartered the US Metric Study, which recommended that the US should follow a careful phasing in of the metric system over the next decade. That led to Congress passing the Metric Conversion Act of 1975 and the formation of the United States Metric Board (USMB) to drive the planning, conversion, and education processes.

The execution almost immediately ran into indifference and resistance. Very little progress was made, and the USMB received little support from either the public or private sector. Tired of treading water, in 1981 the USMB asked Congress for a clear congressional mandate. There was very little appetite in Congress for this. In 1982 the Reagan administration assessed the lack of progress and the cost of migration and decided that it wasn't worth it. The effort to go metric was finally abandoned.

It may be tempting to write off this episode to the proverbial lack of consistent government priorities and professional execution. The fact is, this isn't very different from the tug-of-war and second-guessing that occurs during transformations in most corporations. There was no clear common purpose that could rally the country or the change leaders. Interestingly, there was a financial case for change, but it was hard to understand. The USMB, which led the change in this case, had no air cover from Congress, who were in theory the sponsors of this change. Neither Congress nor the president had any particular skin in the game.

Most digital transformation efforts end up looking remarkably similar to the US metrics project. Let's contrast that with an example of a more successful transformation from recent history.

The Turnaround of the *Washington Post*

Under the surface of the *Washington Post*'s recent turnaround is successful use of technology, driven by the ownership of Amazon founder and CEO Jeff Bezos. The *Washington Post* was in deep trouble in 2013. Revenues were down 7 percent to $581 million in 2012. The paper had just booked a loss of $54 million, up from $21 million in the previous year. Print ad revenue continued to decline. It had dropped by 14 percent in 2012. Circulation of the print edition had also declined 2 percent. They weren't alone; similar iconic newspapers and magazines were also suffering. The *Boston Globe* had just been sold for $70 million. *Newsweek* had been sold for a mere $1 (although with it came the magazine's accumulated financial liabilities). When Jeff Bezos accepted the offer to buy the *Washington Post* for $250 million, opinion was divided on whether this was just a goodwill donation to a storied institution or a smart business decision that was simply not apparent to others.

Fast-forward to 2017. The *Post* announced plans to hire more than sixty journalists after years of layoffs and hiring freezes. The *Post* is privately held, so financial results are not openly published; however *Forbes* reported publisher Fred Ryan sharing with employees that the paper is now "profitable and growing." Subscriptions were reported to have grown 75 percent, and digital subscription revenues doubled. Online web visits surpassed those at the *New York Times* for the first time.

What did Bezos do to revive the *Post*? He set the vision to turn it into a great national and global paper. He supported and provided a high degree of freedom to the editorial side of the business, while dramatically transforming the digital and consumer-centric parts of the newspaper. He put real skin in the game in terms of investments, and he personally participated in much of the technology transformation. The sidebar provides more details on Bezos's actions. In the rest of this chapter, I codify the actions that define systemic support and empowerment on digital transformations.

How the Turnaround of the *Washington Post* Worked

For a person who runs one of the largest retailers in the world and a space exploration company on the side, Jeff Bezos was very hands-on in the operations of the *Washington Post*, especially on the digital transformation.

Bezos set a compelling vision to transform "a great local paper into a great national and global paper." He developed a new digital business model where a large number of users sample the product via social networks and then become repeat purchasers for higher-value products. Bezos then set up a highly empowered set of change leaders behind his strategy. In many ways he has been an editor's dream owner, providing great autonomy editorially, combined with patience on short-term financial outcomes. This strategic patience has allowed the editorial side to flourish while driving the conversion of the paper into a primarily digital publication at the *Post*.

Bezos invested $50 million, mostly in technology and the newsroom. He tripled the size of the engineering team at the *Post*, which now has IT capability that rivals those in technology companies. He has been personally active in the digital side, where engineers are free to contact him. He has pushed for a superior digital user experience with innovations on speed to load pages. The Amazon culture of reducing friction for users in any digital transaction is clearly being applied to digital publications.

One other page that is being borrowed from the Amazon playbook is that the *Post* is now starting to sell its internal tools to other newspapers. The tool is called Arc Publishing. It provides a digital platform for complex publishing needs, including video, mobile web syndication, and data mining, and has more than a dozen clients and is aiming for $100 million in annual revenue. This is similar to the Amazon game plan that spun off internally developed services like Amazon Web Services.

The Discipline of Disruption Empowerment

There is a common thread across the metric system and *Washington Post* stories in that both were disruptive visions. However, only one of them had the MTP, air cover, skin in the game, and a feeder pipeline of initial projects. The disciplined execution of these four items is what I call "disruption empowerment" (see figure 10). It creates the conditions for the change leaders to execute hard transformations. Let's take a deeper look at these four elements.

Massive Transformative Purpose (MTP)

A massive transformative purpose, or MTP, is the higher aspirational purpose of the organization. It differs from traditional vision statements not just in its pithy format but also in the sheer magnitude of the transformation that it declares. The book *Exponential Organizations* by Salim Ismail makes a strong case that this isn't just a Silicon Valley fad. Most exponential organizations appear to have one:

- Google: Organizing the world's information
- XPRIZE: Making the impossible possible
- Microsoft: A computer in every home and on every desk
- Tesla: To accelerate the world's transition to sustainable transport

What's different about the MTP is its ability to generate a pull and to motivate a community to do the nearly impossible. There's almost a sense of manifest destiny that can result from a strong MTP that pulls together the change drivers, voluntary community members, and those affected by the change.

That's why it's important to set up at least a trial MTP at the initial stage of chartering your digital transformation. It's important to capture the hearts and minds and imagination of not just the central team driving the disruption but the larger community and crowd that will be participating. The *Washington Post* employees are no doubt motivated by the goal to go from being a great local paper to a great global paper.

Figure 10 The elements of disruption empowerment

In contrast, in our example of the metric system conversion, there wasn't a similar aspirational goal that captured the imagination of all the stakeholders.

On P&G's Next Generation Services initiative, we set up an exercise at the initiation of the team where we brainstormed through various options for an MTP. We settled on two options: "Free up the employee, for free" and "Disrupt the shared services industry." We chose the latter because we felt that it had a more exciting and larger scope of work that went beyond transforming employee capabilities.

Air Cover to Take Risks and to Fail Forward

Let's put ourselves in the shoes of the transformation leaders for a moment. They have just been picked to work on an exciting but risky venture. Other than the senior executive sponsoring the change, everyone else views their work with a degree of suspicion and fear. The prevailing reward systems and culture are also likely to be headwinds. How do they continue to face this without getting bogged down or incurring unwarranted career risk?

It's the role of the sponsor to not just legitimize their work but to provide them the custom-designed support to smooth potential reactions from the corporate immune system (more on that in chapter 7). The best way to accomplish this is by proactively addressing this with the transformation leaders, anyone affected by the change, and ancillary stakeholders.

The transformation leaders need to understand not just the success criteria but also the principles and behaviors that will be expected of them. Here's an example of what was chosen for the NGS team:

- Speed is more valued than perfection.

- We expect that only 10 percent of the experiments (projects) will be successful and that the team will fail fast for learning purposes on the rest.

- They have free rein to drive change within certain predefined boundaries, and they will be rewarded for taking smart risks.

- There will be a fast escalation and support mechanism to help shield them against noise generated by corporate immune system reactions.

The people affected by the change would also need to understand how they are going to be taken care of through the change. Examples of the types of questions that need to be answered include:

- What are we changing to, and how is this going to be in their best interests (or, at a minimum, have a neutral effect on their interests)?
- What is the role they need to play during the change?
- How will their reward systems be tweaked to support the transformation?

Ancillary stakeholders also play a key role in enabling the transformation. They need to understand where they need to help and where to stay away by providing answers to these questions:

- What is the transformation, and why it is critical?
- What is the role they need to play, and where are they likely to be called in to help?
- What are the enabling signals they need to send to their organizations to support the transformation?

Addressing these questions with the change leaders, the change-affected, and the ancillary stakeholders sets up the necessary reward systems for success. P&G's Global Business Services leadership was very deliberate in enabling this.

The second way in which air cover can be provided is to openly commit to it as an important strategy and to communicate it openly. GBS president Julio Nemeth took on this role enthusiastically. The freedom afforded by such air cover goes a long way to delivering fast and effective transformation. Those entrusted with the US metric conversion project continued to be under attack from some of the members of the same Congress that had chartered them to lead the work. That's the *opposite* of air cover!

Leadership Skin in the Game

As they say, leadership skin in the game is the difference between being involved and being committed, which is like ham and eggs—the chicken was involved, but the pig was committed.

Warren Buffett usually uses the concept in the context of company leaders investing in the companies that they run, and the term is therefore often incorrectly attributed to him. The analogy is perfect for digital change leaders. For enterprise-wide change, the executive leadership, from the owner/leader/CEO downward, needs to have true skin in the game. The difference in skin in the game in the examples of the metric system failure and the *Washington Post* turnaround was clear. Congress had very little skin in the game for the metric system change. And even the little commitment that was there was fully eroded after the change of administrations. By contrast, Bezos has his own money invested at the *Washington Post*, although skin in the game doesn't have to be monetary alone. Personal time investment is equally important. At P&G, the GBS leadership was completely open with their time for the NGS work. I worked out of the same open-office desks as the rest of the team to enable informal meetings and fast decisions. Julio spent several hours each month on the floor. Every GBS sponsor provided weekly input on their projects.

Skin in the game can also come in other ways. It can be an open declaration of commitment to business outcomes. So for instance, in converting advertising to digital platforms instead of the traditional print or TV media, a combination of both dollar amount committed to digital media as well as a commitment to outcomes in hitting certain thresholds in each of the business units will drive the conversion faster than just an overall corporate-level goal.

Feeder Pipeline for Starting Disruption

One of the hardest problems facing the transformation leader is to get momentum going. During the initial days, speed matters a lot. Like crime solving, where the probability of an arrest falls dramatically after the first few days, the lack of momentum can kill digital transformation. The best way to build momentum is to get a quick win. Experienced sponsors know how to prime the pump with a good starter project, something that will generate a quick win and help build momentum. At NGS, we handpicked highly credible operational senior executives from each of the GBS service lines to work full-time in NGS. They were able to identify and seed the first few efforts to transform their previous operations rapidly. Of the batch of four experiments (projects) that were started in the summer of 2015, we were certain that at least one would deliver major quick-win results within three months.

Chapter Summary

- Digital transformation is a hard change. Underinvesting in empowering the transformation leaders is a mistake that often comes back to derail progress.

- The metric conversion effort of 1975 in the US fizzled out in a few years because the change leaders (the United States Metric Board) were not empowered sufficiently by Congress to drive the change.

- In contrast, the editorial board and the technology leaders of the *Washington Post* have witnessed strong commitment and empowerment from owner Jeff Bezos in driving digital transformation.

- To codify disruption empowerment, four elements were identified:

  ▶ **Massive transformative purpose** (MTP)—articulating an ambitious higher-order purpose that motivates and pulls in people to the goal.

  ▶ **Air cover to take risks and to fail fast**—providing the transformation team with the freedom to be a "learn by doing" team.

  ▶ **Leadership skin in the game**—clearly lining up your personal success to the success of the change via a visible level of personal commitment.

  ▶ **Feeder pipeline for starting disruption**—helping the flywheel of transformation get moving by seeding the effort with a quick-win choice of pilot.

Your Disciplines Checklist

Evaluate your digital transformation against the questions in figure 11 to follow a disciplined approach to each step in Digital Transformation 5.0.

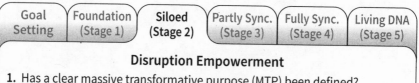

Goal Setting	Foundation (Stage 1)	**Siloed (Stage 2)**	Partly Sync. (Stage 3)	Fully Sync. (Stage 4)	Living DNA (Stage 5)

Disruption Empowerment

1. Has a clear massive transformative purpose (MTP) been defined?
2. Have the change leaders been communicated with about which specific elements of air cover they will receive as they drive change?
3. Have the ancillary stakeholders and the change-affected been informed of their role to help the change?
4. Has the leader identified and committed to having personal skin in the game for the transformation?
5. Has the leader primed the pump for change with a few initiatives to drive the momentum?

Figure 11 Your disciplines checklist for disruption empowerment

Chapter 6

Digital Leverage Points

One of the problems with digital transformation is that digital technology is so ubiquitous that deciding where to leverage it can be a challenge. Following a disciplined approach to address this is possible, as we will see in the following example.

Netflix is probably the best-known serial disruptor in modern corporate history. It has disrupted its own business model at least three times within twenty years (i.e., disrupting store-based rentals with mail-in DVDs and then streaming videos and original content creation) and is now working on its fourth (i.e., leveraging international presence).

What Netflix and other serial disruptors have is the uncanny ability to understand where digital technology can be leveraged the most to create or enable disruptive business models. This is what I call "digital leverage points."

Digital leverage points are simply the best areas where digital technology can be leveraged.

Netflix's Digital Leverage Points

Netflix's multiple disruptions have a few things in common. They are aimed at driving market penetration, along with excellent customer experience and very low costs. Under the surface these are all supported by the company's ability to react quickly to change, its enviable culture, and a consistent willingness to leverage technology to transform its own business model. Those last three items are Netflix's digital leverage points.

Netflix's Record of Repeated Disruptions

What exactly is Netflix? It was founded in 1997 by two software engineers, Reed Hastings and Marc Randolph, to rent DVD movies on the internet. Interestingly, it was previously reported that Hastings had come up with the idea for Netflix after he paid $40 in late fees for an overdue copy of *Apollo 13*. That story has been debunked more recently by Randolph, who said that it was simply a convenient way to explain Netflix's unique model. The origin of the Netflix idea isn't important; it is the ability of the company to keep changing what exactly Netflix is that's relevant.

The first transformation was the replacement of physical movie rental stores by internet and ecommerce-based subscriptions. When they launched in 1998, Netflix had only 925 movie titles. Netflix had apparently offered Blockbuster a partnership in 2000 but was turned down. In an ironic twist, Blockbuster went out of business, mostly thanks to Netflix, in the next five years. The second transformation was in 2007 when Netflix moved to streaming content. For a low monthly fee, subscribers could access a large library of content on demand. The third transformation came with the creation of original content starting with the launch of *The House of Cards* in 2013. And Netflix may be transforming itself again for a fourth time with its international business push.

So, how does Netflix continue its enviable record of serial transformation while most companies struggle to transform their businesses even once? Clearly, there are elements related to leadership and its broader organizational culture that make serial transformation possible. But would that explain how Netflix's transformation is successful in almost all its attempts? The reality is that Netflix is clearly aware of its leverage points of detecting future trends, using its agile culture, and employing cutting-edge technology platforms.

Detect the Disruption Early and Use It

When Netflix was created, all that they wanted to be was the world's largest DVD mailing company. Then Hastings realized that within five years of Netflix's inception, internet bandwidth speeds would grow exponentially. At that pace, the customer experience of ordering DVDs and then waiting a few days to receive them in the mail was going to be disrupted by the instant gratification model of video on demand. The move from mailing DVDs to streaming seems logical today, but it was an extremely bold decision at a time when internet speeds were modest and Netflix's DVD mailing business was flourishing. Today Netflix accounts for a third of all the bandwidth in the US. This ability to detect disruptive forces and leverage them before their competition continues to serve them well.[21]

Culture as a Winning Ingredient

The second leverage point has been Netflix's organization culture, which is legendary. Netflix truly empowers its employees and minimizes processes that are considered normal by other HR organizations. Netflix treats its employees as "fully formed adults." The basic assumption is that its employees want to do the right thing for Netflix, and given the freedom they will deliver their best, taking the appropriate risks to innovate. So, there are no expense reports to be approved, you get unlimited vacation, there are no annual performance reviews, and the compensation packages are lucrative.[22]

Disruptive Technology

The third leverage point is Netflix's technology advantage. Netflix chose an extremely scalable and open technical architecture very early on. Whether optimizing their physical DVD distribution systems or streaming video, they have leveraged their technical foundation as a strength. Netflix converts each film into more than fifty versions to reflect different screen sizes and quality and stores them so that the movie doesn't have to be converted when downloading to match your screen's size and resolution. Interestingly, Netflix hosts its video streaming at Amazon—one of its competitors.[23] This ability to distinguish between a leverage point and a commodity service is strategically important.

■　■　■

In summary, Netflix continues to transform its business models repeatedly by being disciplined in leveraging its strengths of market agility, culture, and technical superiority. Now let's contrast that with a case of an organization that was not as fortunate in understanding its digital leverage points.

The McDonald's "Innovate" Program

In 2001, McDonald's, the international fast-food giant, set about on an ambitious billion-dollar digitization program called "Innovate." They would connect each of their restaurants to their headquarters via a global IT network.[24] The scale of digitization was unprecedented. It would replace their ten-year-old internal systems with an enterprise resource planning software covering human resources, financial management, and supply chain systems. It would provide these back-office capabilities to more than thirty thousand restaurants globally as well as to more than three hundred vendors in real time.

McDonald's intent was laudable. It would use technology to do what it did best—provide the fastest and most consistent service to its customers. However, by 2002, McDonald's had written off $170 million and scrapped the Innovate program.[25]

Innovate was certainly an ambitious idea. However, although technology in itself wasn't the big idea, the project was run as a technology effort. Worse still, store franchisees were already skeptical of corporate IT, since a previous IT implementation had ended up slowing down service. Unlike Netflix, which has proven technology capabilities at its core, technology itself was not a feasible digital leverage point for McDonald's at the time. Instead, the company could have transformed the efficiency of their strong franchisee and vendor models using technology. But that's not how the effort was executed.

There were also issues of cost, excessive scope, and poor execution methodology, but those are secondary to the issue of understanding the leverage points for the transformation. Whatever the issues, McDonald's should get marks for pulling the plug on the project rapidly. The only thing that is worse than a bad project is a bad project that drags on.

Understanding Digital Leverage Points

Digital leverage points are strategic areas within an enterprise where technology has the most *transformational* (i.e., not just automation) impact in the Fourth Industrial Revolution. These are identified through a deep understanding of the organization's opportunities and strategic choices. This is where the major digital transformation bets need to be placed, such as with digital retail (e.g., Walmart), big data (e.g., most health-care providers), user centricity (e.g., Zappos), and so on. Digital leverage points can be internal or external to the enterprise. Placing digital transformation bets on internal capabilities is equally valid, as with highly efficient logistics (e.g., Amazon), R&D (e.g., Intel), supply chain (e.g., Apple), and others.

Digital leverage points are tailored for each enterprise. They differ from those in other industries and may differ from those of competitors.

The challenge with identifying digital leverage points is that it presupposes a certain level of understanding of what digital technology can do. That's the dilemma that most leaders find themselves in. If you're unsure about where disruptive technology can play within your business model, then how do you strategically choose the right areas?

The good news is that there is a deliberate sequence of steps that can be followed here. It doesn't even need new tools or methodologies, as you will note in the following paragraphs. The answer, once again, is discipline. It involves a deliberate approach that starts with "what's needed," then evaluates "what's possible," and finally connects the two using structured creativity. Specifically:

- *Start with business strengths, opportunities, or pain points.* This should link to the normal strategy processes. You can't go too wrong if you're playing with strategic opportunities.

- *Understand the digital possibilities.* Use internal or external experts to understand what digital technology can do relative to the enterprises goals. A basic level of digital literacy helps move this along.

- *Translate strategic strengths, opportunities, and pain points into big ideas that use digital.* Use creative processes to put together digital possibilities with potential strength or opportunity areas. Using approaches such as design thinking can help significantly.

Now, let's look at each of these steps in more depth.

Start with Strategic Strengths, Opportunities, or Pain Points

Disruptive transformation comes from one of three areas in any organization:

- Enabling new business models
- Creating new types of digital product or service offerings
- Transforming operational processes for competitive advantage

The starting point with identifying strategic opportunities. There are several strategy development and renewal processes that can help. One of the favorites is the Business Model Canvas.

The Business Model Canvas (figure 12) was developed by Alexander Osterwalder in 2008 to visually depict and align strategic choices in value proposition, infrastructure, customers, and finances. Inserting digital possibilities into the mix can help you identify potential ideas and tradeoffs in new business models, new business offerings, and transformational operational processes.

Understand the Digital Possibilities

The good news about technology is that it is often more capable than we realize. The bad news is that the devil is in the detail. You need to leverage internal and external resources on where exactly exponential technologies can mesh with the opportunities identified in the previous step. Chapter 10, "Staying Current," helps build this knowledge systemically, but it is possible to address this situationally as well. The key is to understand what the most disruptive technology trends are, as well as to get a firm grasp of their limitations.

As mentioned in chapter 2, institutions such as Singularity University (SU) are masters at identifying future trends. They provide insights into the amazing future but use current tangible examples, which can help trigger other ideas. After all, "the future is already here—it's just not very evenly distributed" as William Ford Gibson, a science fiction writer who has been called the "noir prophet" of cyberpunk fiction, is reputed to have said. Getting into specific cases where the "future is already here" helps tremendously.

To offer some examples, in several large cities a technology called ShotSpotter uses sensors and algorithms to pinpoint the location of gunshots fired to within ten meters accuracy, in real time. Robots are used in the Middle East as jockeys for camel racing. The power of networked computing continues to explode. Ten years ago, about five hundred thousand computing devices were connected globally in a network. By 2020 that number will be more than fifty billion. Meanwhile the power of individual computers continues to skyrocket. Today's average phone chip does a billion calculations per second and is the most expensive component in the phone. By 2020, that component will cost just one penny. Meanwhile AI continues to get more and

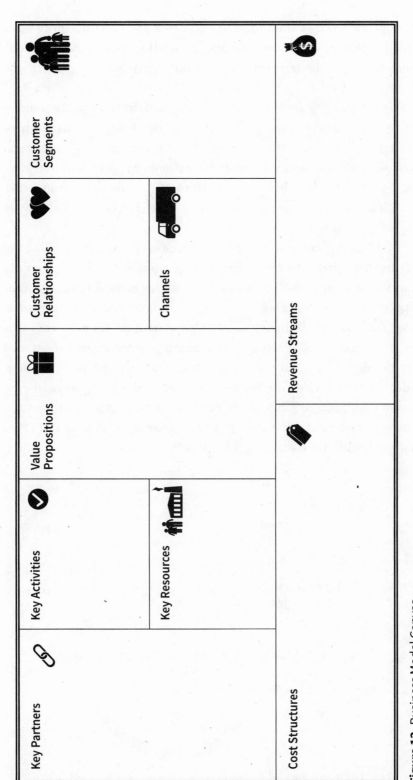

Figure 12 Business Model Canvas

more powerful. It is used to scan tax forms and to write short news updates. Similarly, software robotics is starting to replace many offshore resources in business process outsourcing (BPO). That's the future that is already here.

To balance the review of future possibilities, it's equally important to understand the limitations of these technologies. That's where trusted technical experts can help. To illustrate this with a general example—when leveraging disruptive technology, it's critical to understand that technology has only one-third of the power when it comes to digital transformation. There are two other forces that multiply its impact (see figure 13).

The first is exponential processes, which is all about eliminating the intermediary parts of work processes to jump directly to the outcomes in as few steps as possible. One example of this is the idea of customer support call centers. Despite Amazon's ubiquitous retail presence, how often do we call their customer support line? It's a process that has been almost eliminated by redesigning order management and logistics operations and providing full visibility to customers on their orders as self-service. The second force multiplier is exponential ecosystems. Airbnb and Uber would not have gotten very far without the sharing economy and the ability to tap into an ecosystem of resources that multiplied the assets available to them.

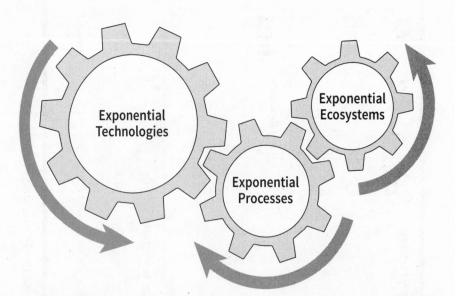

Figure 13 The multiplier effect of technology plus process plus ecosystems

Together, these three capabilities multiply the possibilities when it comes to digital transformation.

Technology Limitations: Why Technology Is Only One-Third of the Disruption

Understanding the possibilities of digital technologies is more involved than understanding their technical capabilities. The interplay of exponential technologies, exponential work processes, and exponential ecosystems can deliver massive transformations beyond what individual technologies can offer. Exponential work processes and ecosystems can multiply the effects of technology.

Exponential Technologies: Exponential technologies are the most disruptive capabilities possible because they show exponential promise. Although the exponential performance concept originally came from the doubling of the price-performance ratio of computers every eighteen months, the idea has been broadened to include all technologies with disruptive capabilities. This includes, among others, AI, machine learning, nanotechnology, 3D printing, the Internet of Things (IoT), robotics, synthetic biology, and biotech. In corporate settings, newer technology is transforming the way businesses are run. Imagine virtual assistants operating self-service contact centers in the future. Many brokerages are starting to leverage virtual financial advisors. Natural language generators and machine learning are automatically writing financial or sports update articles in real time. Algorithms are beginning to hyperpersonalize and recommend orders to customers.

However, exponential technology is only one-third of the equation.

Exponential Work Processes: Exponential technologies are at their powerful best when used to reimagine work processes as opposed to automating existing ones. We have seen this in action already—just think of the change in the movie rental process from Blockbuster's in-store movie rentals to Netflix's first mail-in DVD offering. What used to take a trip to the store to check out a DVD took a different activity system, i.e. no trip necessary. The outcome (movie rental) was the same. The work processes needed to deliver it were very different.

Exponential Ecosystems: The final multiplier is the ability to tap into an unlimited number of resources using ecosystems of people and technical assets. You can now hire almost any skilled resource—from lawyers to cybersecurity services—via certified crowd services. There is also a growing list of assets as services available on demand, from software to extra trucking logistics capacity.

Translate Strategic Opportunities and Pain Points Into Big Ideas

The final step is to bring together strategic opportunities and digital possibilities using creative ideation processes. This is more than an exercise in automating the identified opportunities using digital technology. That would be called digitalization (which is the process of automating a task using digital technologies), not digital transformation (which seeks to reinvent the game using digital). Think of the difference this way—while major hotel chains were busy coming up with automated and mobile-based check-in systems in the early 2000s, Airbnb quietly eliminated the whole idea of a check-in desk. True digital transformation requires not just automation but reimagination.

The best tool that I have come across for the purpose is design thinking. The human-centric approach, the ability to generate many ideas quickly using brainstorming, and the ability to turn abstract ideas into tangible prototypes and to test them all make design thinking an ideal tool to frame the big idea (see sidebar).[26] Tools like design thinking use the power of creativity to blend together the business opportunities identified in the first step and the disruptive technology trends of the second into a coherent set of digital leverage points.

In summary, digital leverage points are the best transformation choices made possible by digital technologies, processes, and ecosystems. Turning digital leverage points into big ideas is a key discipline for successful transformation. The simple three-step process described above first identifies strategic leverage points, then understands digital possibilities, and finally uses design thinking–type techniques to come up with the big idea.

How Design Thinking Can Be Used in Real Life: Bank of America's "Keep the Change" Program

"Design thinking is a design methodology that provides a solution-based approach to solving problems. It's extremely useful in tackling complex problems that are ill-defined or unknown," according to the Interaction Design Foundation, a leading design thinking education nonprofit. Though design thinking has been popular with product designers and other creative experts for a while, it is now being used in many different circles.

The "Keep the Change" program from Bank of America is an excellent example of design thinking. In 2004, the company hired a design firm to help identify innovative ideas to encourage boomer-age women to open more bank accounts. The team did extensive research, including following members of their target audience to learn their habits and practices.

At the end of that, they stumbled upon two insights. First, they discovered that boomer-age women had a hard time saving. In many cases it was due to a lack of a routine to help facilitate saving. The second insight was that people seemed to round up their transactions because it was easier for them. This eventually led to the creation of the "Keep the Change" program that was launched in late 2005. The idea was simple. Customers with a Bank of America debit card could choose to round up the charge for any purchase and move the rounded-up portion of the charge to a separate savings account. Bank of America also matched the rounded-up amount for a period of three months and up to 5 percent of the annual spending up to $250 annually. By 2010, the idea had generated ten million new customers and helped their clients save $1.8 billion.

Chapter Summary

- Leverage points are essentially your strategic strengths and opportunities that best leverage digital. You identify these using a deep understanding of your organization's business opportunities and strategies.

- Leverage points need to be translated into big ideas for digital transformation. The three steps involved are as follows:
  - ▶ Start with your strategic opportunities or pain points.
  - ▶ Understand the digital possibilities.
    - ◆ There is a perfect storm of exponential technologies, exponential processes, and exponential ecosystems that can be used to disrupt just about any area.
  - ▶ Translate your strategic opportunities and pain points into big ideas that use digital.
    - ◆ Design thinking is an excellent tool to come up with new, breakthrough ideas, even in complex situations.

Your Disciplines Checklist

Evaluate your digital transformation against the questions in figure 14 to follow a disciplined approach to each step in Digital Transformation 5.0.

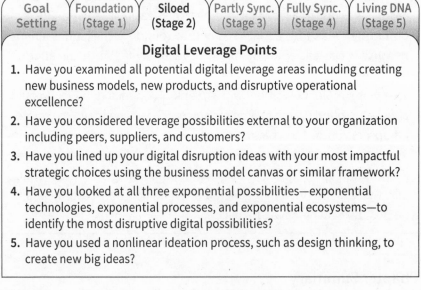

Goal Setting	Foundation (Stage 1)	**Siloed (Stage 2)**	Partly Sync. (Stage 3)	Fully Sync. (Stage 4)	Living DNA (Stage 5)

Digital Leverage Points

1. Have you examined all potential digital leverage areas including creating new business models, new products, and disruptive operational excellence?
2. Have you considered leverage possibilities external to your organization including peers, suppliers, and customers?
3. Have you lined up your digital disruption ideas with your most impactful strategic choices using the business model canvas or similar framework?
4. Have you looked at all three exponential possibilities—exponential technologies, exponential processes, and exponential ecosystems—to identify the most disruptive digital possibilities?
5. Have you used a nonlinear ideation process, such as design thinking, to create new big ideas?

Figure 14 Your disciplines checklist for digital leverage points

Stage 3

Partially Synchronized

What Is Stage 3?	Partial completion of an enterprise-wide strategy for digital transformation. The term "partially" in the title is reflective of part business-outcome delivery, not part synchronization of efforts.
Causes of Failure	An ineffective change management strategy or insufficient amount of transformation projects to adequately transform the core organization.
Disciplines to Address Risks	▪ *Change management model* for effectively transforming the core organization. ▪ *Strategy sufficiency* in terms of the portfolio of initiatives needed to drive a complete transformation.

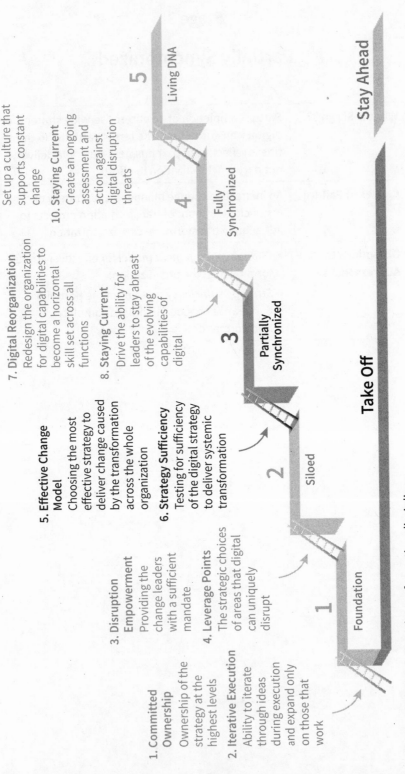

1. Committed Ownership
   Ownership of the strategy at the highest levels

2. Iterative Execution
   Ability to iterate through ideas during execution and expand only on those that work

3. Disruption Empowerment
   Providing the change leaders with a sufficient mandate

4. Leverage Points
   The strategic choices of areas that digital can uniquely disrupt

5. Effective Change Model
   Choosing the most effective strategy to deliver change caused by the transformation across the whole organization

6. Strategy Sufficiency
   Testing for sufficiency of the digital strategy to deliver systemic transformation

7. Digital Reorganization
   Redesign the organization for digital capabilities to become a horizontal skill set across all functions

8. Staying Current
   Drive the ability for leaders to stay abreast of the evolving capabilities of digital

9. Agile Culture
   Set up a culture that supports constant change

10. Staying Current
    Create an ongoing assessment and action against digital disruption threats

Foundation   Siloed   Partially Synchronized   Fully Synchronized   Living DNA

1   2   3   4   5

Take Off

Stay Ahead

Figure 15 Stage 3 digital transformation disciplines

Chapter 7

Effective Change Model

As a consumer, I hate call centers that force me to talk to robots. I find it frustrating to have to work through a long menu of options for support with robots, especially when their voice recognition is poor. (Or is it possible that I have a blind tendency to discriminate against robots, for which I will pay dearly when they become our overlords in the future? I'm kidding!) In any case, I was genuinely surprised in 2015 when our new NGS team found that AI-based call center support was a major disruptive focus among start-ups. As it happened, we were looking for 10X improvement solutions for our Global Consumer Relations service, which provides phone, email, and social media support to all consumers of P&G products worldwide. We established an NGS project and ran through a quick cycle of hypothesis testing with the technologies in four weeks that demonstrated that it was a very viable 10X idea.

Two months later, we killed this effort. The technology was indeed viable, and the service line leaders in GBS were clearly sponsoring the effort, but the project was not making satisfactory progress within their core operating organization. The kill decision was based on our NGS portfolio approach of 10-5-4-1, where for every ten experiments (projects), we would stop five, expect four to deliver 2X results, and one would become a huge 10X hit. Over the next three years we would similarly kill dozens of potentially viable projects. Ninety percent of the time the issue was not technology viability but a lack of sufficient progress within the receiving operating organization. In all these cases, our goal was to stop the effort as early as possible, to recognize the "kill decision" publicly, and to move on.

Two years later, the conditions within the Global Consumer Relations organization had changed, and so the old project was revived. It is currently turning out to be one of the most successful efforts in the current portfolio.

Change Management Is a Major Failure Point for Stage 3 Transformation

Change management is tough at any stage, but it is the most likely cause of failure at Stage 3 even among strong, well-intentioned enterprises. Even though the transformation strategy has been declared, the change never seems to take root in the core organization.

Work backward from change acceptance strategies toward change creation, not the other way around.

Past experience with disruptive innovation at GBS had led us to a different way of thinking about effective change management in NGS. We decided that our operating model ought to work backward from change acceptance toward change (product) creation, as opposed to the traditional approach of creating the product first and then figuring out how to drive acceptance along the way. Here's one simple example of how this insight was used. In deciding on whether to locate the NGS team in Silicon Valley or at P&G HQ in Cincinnati, I chose the latter. I determined it would be in the best interests of driving change into the core operations for the team to be based there.

In this chapter, I explore how choosing an effective change model can be done in a disciplined manner. In essence, this consists of three parts:

- Understand your change situation transformation (e.g., burning platform, proactive change, etc.).

- Choose the appropriate change management model for it (e.g., organic change, inorganic change, etc.).

- Create plans to motivate those affected by the change.

To illustrate how this works, let's investigate a couple of case studies for insights before using them for our change-model discipline. Let's go back in time to the case study of the Year 2000 (Y2K) global effort. Our younger readers may have only a fleeting knowledge of this, but the Y2K problem was a very big deal in the 1990s. At a time when IT was not the consumer phenomenon that it is today, it caused a barely understood topic to hit the front pages for a frightening reason—this problem could cause all types of real-world disasters to happen.

Why the Global Y2K Fix Effort Succeeded

The Y2K computer glitch story may be the biggest example of successful global collaboration on an IT issue in our lifetime. The issue boiled down to twentieth-century programming practices where the storage of a number representing a year (e.g., 1998) was often done in two digits (e.g., 98). The program treated any computation that involved a year—say computing the number representing "next year"—by simple mathematical action against that number (e.g., 98 + 1 = 99). That worked perfectly for most of the twentieth century. The problem arose when the computations gave you a three-digit result (e.g., 99 + 1 = 100). Most programs failed when they tried to store a three-digit result in a two-digit number.

There was also a smaller secondary issue with leap years, where computer programmers incorrectly coded leap years in the Gregorian calendar. They simply programmed any year divisible by 100 as not being a leap year, forgetting that the exception was for years divisible by 400. Thus, the year 2000 should have been programmed as a leap year.

The problem was easy to explain, but the fix was easier said than done. There was no easy way to find out which specific programs were incorrectly coded with two-digit years as opposed to the correct four-digit years. Worse still, many of the original programs would have been modified locally, with little to no documentation of the changes. You'd have to go through each and every program and fix it.

In the end the new millennium dawned and passed without incident. Somehow in the last remaining years of the twentieth century, governments and business leaders took charge and delivered their individual fixes. Keep in mind that these were the days when IT was not fully understood by most organization leaders and stakeholders. Even so, without fully understanding the cause of the problem, most leaders were clear about what success looked like.

Y2K—An Example of Crisis Change Management

The Y2K issue was first noticed in the 1980s and was the subject of an influential book, *Computers in Crisis* by Jerome and Marilyn Murray, published in 1984. Usenet groups that preceded the modern internet quickly caught onto this issue, and by the '90s, various degrees of panic had spread around the world. Although nobody could accurately predict the exact nature of the impact, the possible scenarios were all bad. Airplanes might fall out of the sky, banks could see inaccurate transactions, national security programs might be affected, and business operations might be heavily disrupted. For a change, governments, corporations, and the public were unanimous in their desire for action.

The only way to fix the issue would be for literally every IT organization in the world to set aside other priorities and assume accountability to fix the programs that they ran. By the time most people realized this, it was already the late 1990s. Meanwhile, the clock ticked inexorably toward the millennium. Fixing the problem would take an unprecedented concerted effort across the whole world. This had never been attempted on such a huge scale, outside of movie fiction where the entire world quickly comes together against an impending doomsday scenario like an alien invasion or an approaching asteroid.

The Y2K fix is a fascinating example of decentralized execution of a common global issue. Every enterprise that had an IT capacity had a Y2K project. The work was messy, it was hard at times, and yet most IT professionals who worked on Y2K projects consider the experience to have been among the most enjoyable of their careers. The mandate was clear, the work was hard but rewarding, there was a clear sense of purpose, and failure was not a pleasant option. And so, the messiest IT project of the twentieth century—one that was mostly uncoordinated and decentralized—turned out to be the world's most successful IT change management story.

Crisis-like collaboration has been studied extensively as a sociological phenomenon. It provides excellent insights on how to generate positive change motivation for digital transformation.

The Y2K fix is a good example of working backward from change demand toward change supply. Billions of people across the world wanted this to happen. Every organization knew exactly what it had to do, regardless of what others chose to do. The effort is also a good example of the sociological phenomena underpinning crisis-like change, i.e., there are hidden extra reserves that kick in when facing an existential threat.

To be clear, the goal isn't to frame a digital transformation in crisis terms. Such extra reserves can also be called upon when there's a very exciting opportunity as well. The story of how P&G's Global Business Services tapped into those reserves to help with the humungous effort needed to integrate Gillette into P&G in 2005 brings this point to life. That story is not related to the main NGS example, but it is one of the best examples of how to create the conditions for successful change management that I have come across.

P&G's Integration of Gillette

In January 2005, Procter & Gamble announced that it would acquire Gillette for $57 billion. This was P&G's largest acquisition by far. The company that was a household name globally—with products such as Tide/Ariel, Pantene, Pampers, Bounty, Oil of Olay, and Vicks, among others—would add more iconic brands such as Gillette, Duracell, and Braun.

Filippo Passerini, P&G's visionary president of Global Business Services and IT, looked at this as an opportunity. He thought he could run the combined IT-related services of both companies without increasing the head count or spending above P&G's current numbers. Further, since P&G wanted to aim at exceeding Wall Street expectations about the acquisition, Passerini proposed to integrate all the IT systems within eighteen months.

Ultimately, Passerini did just that. P&G exceeded not just cost synergy targets but also delivered them ahead of the committed schedule. What went into delivering these outstanding results is very instructive with regards to deliberately creating environments where change is accepted.

To create a common and tangible sense of purpose for the entire company, Passerini computed that each day's delay on integration would mean a $3 million loss in cost synergies. This ended up being the capstone piece on change management. It drove a real sense of urgency across the enterprise.

Second, although Passerini took a personal risk to commit to the goals up front and execute the change with highly visible and structured delivery, this created momentum that made it somewhat difficult for the usual change-resistance inertia to take root.

Each wave of systems change was executed with excellence. Any problems that arose during systems changeovers were swiftly dealt with by people manning "Hypercare" centers who ensured that there was no business interruption. What resulted was an industry success story on how to integrate the systems of an acquisition swiftly and successfully.

Having been involved in both the Y2K effort at P&G as well as the integration of Gillette's systems as P&G's CIO, it was fascinating for me to compare the change management models across the two. Despite having very different drivers of change, they both created equally effective change-acceptance motivations. I describe in the following sections how it is possible for leaders to read the prevailing landscape using a simple change framework and create strong motivations for change in the organization.

P&G's Integration of Gillette: A Motivated Change Management Story

Acquisitions are always a gamble, with 70 to 90 percent of all mergers and acquisitions being unsuccessful. Integrating the systems and processes of acquired companies is as tough as complex digital transformations. They have several things in common: they both involve maintaining a core of stable operations while dramatically transforming them, and they are both examples of tough change management. P&G's integration of Gillette's systems was exceptional in the disciplined manner by which the change was driven.

Warren Buffett, the largest shareholder at Gillette, called the acquisition a "dream deal." It would combine P&G, a company with a portfolio that was skewed toward creating delightful products for women, with Gillette, a company that leaned more toward men's products. Having said that, this was a bold move on P&G's part. P&G's stock fell a modest 2 percent upon the announcement. Ultimately, the deal would be considered a success only if the cost-reduction synergies were delivered. As is usually the case, the deal financials assumed both cost and revenue synergies, but cost synergies tend to be more tangible in the short term. P&G had committed to delivering cost synergies of more than $1 billion a year starting within three years. This implied that the combined operations, especially those in supporting functions, would be able to operate in a significantly leaner fashion. So, integrating systems and processes was critical.

However, this would be a daunting task. Gillette wasn't small—it was a global company with annual revenues above $10 billion annually.

Filippo Passerini, P&G's Global Business Services president and CIO, made a bold bet. He committed that P&G could run both companies' processes with no increase to P&G's current spending or head count. The question was, how would we execute this?

The first step was to declare this as a goal and to make the work an unquestionable top priority. Within days of the acquisition it was announced internally that the Gillette integration project would supersede all current and proposed IT and shared services priorities. This meant that all other P&G business requirements for new capabilities were immediately dropped or significantly reduced.

Second, Passerini set about personally handpicking the people who would be part of the Gillette integration project. Traditional assignment-planning lead times were put aside. It was understood that once people were tapped, they would be freed up immediately.

Third, the IT technical strategy was firmly aligned between the two companies within days of the announcement. P&G already had enviable global standard systems—a single SAP system for all its global operations, a design that is out of reach for most organizations even today. Gillette would move to P&G's SAP system. CEO A. G. Lafley supported this fully, declaring that "silly debates" would not be entertained.

Fourth, a clear structure was established to manage decision making related to the integration. At the highest level, the Gillette CEO and the P&G CFO would lead the integration board. Every leadership role in the integration structure was set up in a "two in a box" model, with one person each from Gillette and P&G.

Finally, Passerini set up a rigorous project management structure. He personally picked a young but highly talented GBS leader to lead the whole integration effort. The project leader quickly structured the integration outcomes into three waves. Milestones for when IT, HR, financial, order management, and manufacturing systems would be "cut over" were quickly cast in stone. Objections on schedule were politely but firmly handled. The disciplined rigor in execution paid off as the integration of systems ended up becoming a best-in-class success story.

The Discipline of Understanding the Change Conditions

When it comes to understanding why the change models worked, the first story of the Y2K fixes is easier to understand than the second one of the integration of Gillette systems. After all, the world was facing a disaster scenario. And yet, the Gillette systems integration project successfully created an environment that was not too dissimilar to the global crisis Y2K project. How do change leaders tap into the same organization energy reserves in noncrisis situations?

It is important to sense the right change situation (i.e., change urgency vs. acceptance) and, if necessary, even create specific types of change situations through strong leadership, communication, and discipline.

Strong change leaders create these conditions intuitively. But there is some science behind this. It all hinges on understanding the landscape and applying the right change management models. Strong change leaders understand how much support they have not just at the sponsor level but also with those affected by the change. They understand the prevailing culture of the organization and the type of communication that will be most productive. I use a simple model in figure 16 that maps the urgency of change to the prevailing change acceptance culture, to illustrate this effect. Crisis situations are easier to diagnose and therefore make it easier to choose the right change model. The perceived urgency of the situation typically overrides most other considerations, including change culture. The Y2K fix crisis fell into this category.

The P&G integration of Gillette was a little trickier. It was not a business crisis, and there were different motivations involved, including balancing stability with change. The successful strategy employed there was to create a cultural effect of "welcoming change" by using the motivation systems of the organization. By putting together a proposal for a common goal to meet and exceed external expectations and combining it with a rigorous organizing and accountability framework for every player (including putting a dollar value to delays like Passerini did), a common purpose and sense of urgency was created. The point is that it is important to sense the right change situation and, if necessary, even create specific types of change situations (e.g., urgent change, exciting future change, etc.) through strong leadership, communication, and discipline.

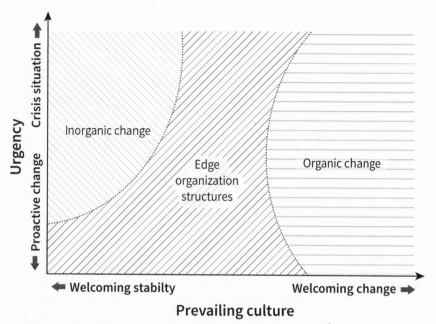

Figure 16 Change situations

The Discipline of Using the Correct Change Model

Once the change management situation has been identified per figure 16, the next step is to decide whether to drive change organically, via edge organization structures, or inorganically, all of which are defined below. An edge organization is a structure that distributes knowledge and power to the "edges" of an organization, enabling it freedom to innovate.[27] If time, capability, and a relatively straightforward digital change per figure 16 are available, then it can usually be handled via organic change. Otherwise you're looking at edge organization structures or inorganic change.

Organic Change

Organic change involves internally setting digital transformation goals, building or buying the right capabilities, educating the organization, and setting the right project execution structures. GE's execution of its well-known digital strategy of creating a separate division called GE Digital is an example of organic change. Though its strategy to become a data company has failed at the moment, that is more related to two other disciplines (iterative execution and strategy sufficiency).

An approach to expediting organic change is to implement the technologies, behaviors, and processes of an exponential organization

(ExO). An ExO essentially uses new organizational techniques that leverage exponential technologies. Inherent in these techniques is the use of nimble, open-team setups and rapid decision making, combined with exponential tools such as algorithms or crowdsourcing.

Edge Organization Structures

If there is little time available and the prevailing organization culture is resistant (even if not closed) to change, then organic change won't work. In such cases, edge organizations that involve creating separate disruptive innovation structures are the preferred approach. Edge organizations are a relatively new construct with great promise for driving change. These organizations consist of highly extended and unconstrained teams that are agile in creating and adapting to change. The charge to apply this concept to large enterprises has been led by John Hagel III, one of the best enterprise change experts I have come across. The legendary example of edge organizations is the original Skunk Works. The Skunk Works group was set up at Lockheed Martin in 1943 as an independent structure that was allowed great freedom from normal processes and rules so that they could develop the XP-80 jet fighter in record time. This type of edge organization works only if it is given full freedom to operate differently than the core.

Inorganic Change

If existing capabilities, time, and internal resistance to change are all a challenge, then your best bet may be to look for an acquisition or partnership with an external entity. Walmart's acquisition of Jet.com is a good example. Inorganic change comes with its own risk since a majority of acquisition-related change fails. However, by giving the acquired entity a strong mandate and change-management support, this approach can jump-start new capabilities quickly.

For additional reading, Salim Ismail's book *Exponential Organizations*[28] has an excellent chapter on this topic: "ExOs for Large Organizations." It provides great detail on four strategic options that mirror our spectrum of organic change, disruptive structures, and inorganic change.

Choosing the most appropriate change model will get the digital transformation off to a strong start. However, to maintain ongoing momentum, there's usually an immune system to be overcome.

Follow the discipline of choosing the best change model (i.e., organic change, edge organization structures, or inorganic change) for your situation.

The Science of Immune System Management

A corporate immune system is not necessarily a bad thing. Like its counterpart in the human body, it plays a vital role. In our bodies, the immune system protects us from disease and keeps us healthy. It is true that immune system disorders can be problematic (i.e., an immune system deficiency leaves the body susceptible to constant infections, while an overactive immune system will fight healthy tissues). However, on balance, a healthy immune system is desirable.

If that's true, then why do so many change leaders blame the corporate immune system when things go south? Shouldn't disciplined change leaders understand the strength of the immune system within their own organizations and prepare for appropriate handling?

For each of the twenty-five experiments (projects) that the NGS team executed during my three years, there was always a proactive immune system conversation and plan. It made a huge difference versus historical trends on disruptive change acceptance.

There are three key principles to bear in mind:

- The immune system is not necessarily a bad thing. Anticipate and prepare for immune system responses.

- Immune system responses can originate at all levels in the organization, but the toughest ones occur at middle management.

- The bigger the change, the harder the immune system response (i.e., digital transformation will be tough).

Having covered the first item, let's zero in on the issue of middle management reaction. In most organizations, it is easy to get senior executive leadership excited about change. Similarly, the younger generation gets quickly on board. It is the middle management layer that's on the critical path and has the potential to slow down or even block change. The term "frozen middle" has been associated with this phenomenon. This concept was published in a *Harvard Business Review* article in 2005 by Jonathan Bynes.[29] Bynes's point was that the most important thing a CEO could do to boost company performance was to build the capabilities of middle management.

For corporate immune system disorders at the middle management level, the term "frozen middle" is accurate, but it comes with the risk of being pejorative for seeming to blame middle management for recalcitrance and inertia. In reality, the responsibility to bring middle management along on the journey resides with the change leaders and their sponsors. Consider this—the so-called frozen middle protects the enterprise from unnecessary distractions and change, just like the human immune system protects the body from harmful change. Middle managers are rewarded mostly for running stable operations. Is it fair to criticize them as a whole for doing what their reward system dictates? We must separate immune system disorders from normal immune system responses.

Pay special attention to creating the reward systems for middle managers to successfully enable the change.

At NGS, we paid special attention to identifying, by name, the middle management leader for each affected project. A lot of effort was put in up front to enroll them, including working with their leaders to tweak their reward systems in order to encourage leadership on the change project. In the few cases that were likely to fall in the category of an immune system disorder, the sponsor was roped in to develop appropriate motivation systems. Worst case, if that didn't work, was that the project was quickly killed. That worked well because of the portfolio effect of having several other projects available in the pipeline.

Why the Frozen Middle Is Especially Important in Digital Transformations

Though the concept of a frozen middle is applicable broadly, overcoming it has never been as critical as it is with digital disruption. The amount of change necessitated by a true Stage 5 transformation is massive. This isn't just a technology or product or process change but also an organizational culture change. The middle management will need to lead the rest of the organization in learning new capabilities (i.e., digital) as well as new ways of working in the digital era, including encouraging agility, taking risk, and re-creating entire new business models and internal processes. Retraining middle management on digital possibilities is not sufficient. Entirely new reward systems and organizational processes will be called for.

Chapter Summary

- Although every airplane takeoff plans for headwinds, most digital transformations treat it as an afterthought. The discipline of addressing the choices of effective change models is designed to address this.

- To understand how successful change management works, this chapter included a couple of success stories—the global Y2K fix and the highly successful systems integration of Gillette into Procter & Gamble.

- There are disciplined steps involved in selecting the best change models. The first is a clear understanding of the organization's change conditions.

- Based on the change situation, three types of change management strategies are available for digital transformation:
  - ▶ **Organic change**
  - ▶ **Edge organization structures**
  - ▶ **Inorganic change**

- Finally, the discipline of addressing the reward systems of the corporate frozen middle proactively builds capabilities and culture at the middle management layer to accept and thrive in digital transformation.

Your Disciplines Checklist

Evaluate your digital transformation against the questions in figure 17 to follow a disciplined approach to each step in Digital Transformation 5.0.

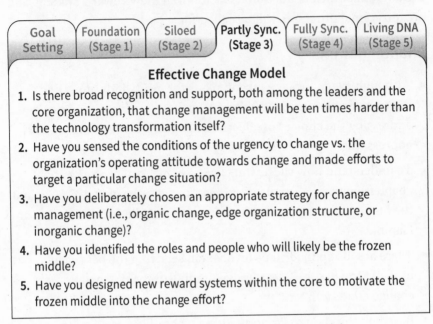

| Goal Setting | Foundation (Stage 1) | Siloed (Stage 2) | Partly Sync. (Stage 3) | Fully Sync. (Stage 4) | Living DNA (Stage 5) |

Effective Change Model

1. Is there broad recognition and support, both among the leaders and the core organization, that change management will be ten times harder than the technology transformation itself?

2. Have you sensed the conditions of the urgency to change vs. the organization's operating attitude towards change and made efforts to target a particular change situation?

3. Have you deliberately chosen an appropriate strategy for change management (i.e., organic change, edge organization structure, or inorganic change)?

4. Have you identified the roles and people who will likely be the frozen middle?

5. Have you designed new reward systems within the core to motivate the frozen middle into the change effort?

Figure 17 Your disciplines checklist for effective change model

Chapter 8

Strategy Sufficiency

I discovered a passion for stock market trading six months before the big dot-com crash in March 2000. Online trading tools were growing dramatically in capability. I tentatively bought a few tech stocks, and within a few weeks they had doubled in value. Hmm, I thought, that's encouraging; I should invest some more. I knew the looming risks of a market downturn and so decided on a couple of mutual funds instead of individual stocks for my next investment, which was much bigger. Three months later, the dot-com bubble burst and my total holding ended up at about half the value of my original investments. The mutual funds hadn't been diverse enough. Thankfully, I hadn't put too much into the stock market in total. However, it was still a painful lesson on the virtues of portfolio management.

Good financial portfolio management, as you know, starts with a targeted goal for return on investment by a specified end date. And then it involves creating a mix of diversified holdings, including high-, medium-, and low-risk components, to maximize the chance of hitting the goal, despite headwinds and economic cycles. It's a proven model that works for retail investors. Which leads us to a more relevant question: Why don't most digital transformations run as disciplined portfolios too?

Digital Transformation Portfolio Sufficiency

The financial portfolio management discipline applies to digital transformation perfectly. It is possible to define an end goal, such as a certain percentage of your business being run on totally new digital business models by a given date. Next, leverage the mix effect by combining high- and low-risk projects optimally. And finally, generate a sufficient number of projects to run through this portfolio—enough to transform the desired percentage of your enterprise. I call this approach "strategy sufficiency."

The NGS portfolio process was designed exactly this way and will be described at the end of the chapter. First, it would help to reflect on why we don't see more examples of strategy sufficiency. The short answer is that there can be a misguided emphasis on driving change enthusiasm in the organization without the requisite portfolio rigor.

Innovation Theater Is the Enemy of Strategy Sufficiency

The discipline of checking for both a sufficient portfolio mix and the requisite volume of projects is at the core of strategy sufficiency. The opposite of this is a plan that relies too heavily on sheer enthusiasm. Don't get me wrong—enthusiasm about change is vital. Where things start to fall apart is when it is not backed up by disciplined execution. If a digital transformation seems a bit heavy on any of the following six activities, then it might be time to bring in the rigor.

- *Silicon Valley's Mecca tours*—a few days spent in business-casual dress marveling at the magical offerings of start-ups. Or spent in the glassed-in innovation centers of the larger tech companies offering "inspiration workshops" on your problems.

- *Lonely innovation planet outpost*—staffing a few people in global innovation hub locations, free from the stifling headquarters bureaucracy, but quickly forgotten or ignored by the core organization.

- *Internal crowdsourcing drama*—the earnest attempts to collect innovation ideas from within the company, or the attempted one-off hackathons, without the wherewithal to execute them.

- *Outsourced innovation delusion*—the hiring of highly paid consultants to take accountability for inspiration, iterative execution, and external solution connections. It's a start, except that true perpetual transformation cannot be outsourced.

- *Labs for chasing cool technologies*—the misguided attempt to focus on shiny object technologies without clarity on the problems to be solved.

- *Highly delegated souls innovation group*—the group of junior resources flailing in their attempt to do their best to drive the hardest of changes in the company.

Granted, elements of these tactics have a role to play in a successful disruptive transformation program. However, the haphazard application of these tactics does not lead to a sufficient strategy for digital transformation.

Innovation theater is the opposite of strategy sufficiency.

What delivers strategy sufficiency is a strong portfolio mix and the right input project volume, which I expand upon in the coming sections using the examples of Alphabet/Google for portfolio mix and the Virgin Group for generating the right volume of input ideas. These are organizations to which a fertile innovation culture comes natively. Somewhere along their early growth cycle, they recognized that their best business strategy was one of constant change. How they got there isn't important. We just need to unbundle their discipline and get to the essence that can be transplanted into other organizations.

Alphabet/Google's Formula for a Sufficient Mix of Transformative Ideas

Google has always had an entrepreneurial mindset as its lifeblood since inception, but ex-CEO Eric Schmidt gets credit for making transformation systemic via a portfolio mix of work that includes big-bet ideas and incremental improvement ideas in addition to daily operations.

A healthy mix is important—if the list of ideas is weighted too heavily toward incremental change or toward highly risky ideas, the outcome degrades. A good mix includes ideas that improve daily operations, those that enable continuous evolution, and game-changing disruptive ideas, or 10X as they are called, for delivering ten times the impact as opposed to 10 percent improvements. Eric Schmidt advocated for a mix of these, roughly in the 70-20-10 ratio.

The 70-20-10 Mix for Sufficiency of Transformation

The formula that Google came up with is a 70-20-10 ratio of employee capacity for innovation.[30] Specifically,

- 70 percent of people's capacity is *dedicated* to core business

- 20 percent of their capacity is *related* to a core project

- 10 percent of their capacity is spent on *unrelated* new businesses

The key was to create a platform where employees could take systemic risks, thrive in ambiguity, and be encouraged to come up with prototypes rather than slides. Ideas had to be original. The culture had to promote "yes" rather than "no." It had to feed the core business while also encouraging hugely disruptive 10X ideas.

Setting up and professionally managing a sufficient portfolio of projects delivers sufficient and scaled digital transformation.

To be clear, the 70-20-10 ratio isn't a universal formula for all innovation portfolios. The generic idea, however, has sound roots. In a *Harvard Business Review* article in May 2012 titled "Managing Your Innovation Portfolio,"[31] Geoff Tuff and Bansi Nagji reported that a study of companies in the manufacturing, technology, and consumer goods sectors revealed that those that allocated 70 percent of their innovation activity to core initiatives, 20 percent to adjacent ones, and 10 percent to transformational ones outperformed their peers via a price-to-earnings premium of 10 to 20 percent. What these organizations were able to do was not just strike the ideal balance of core, adjacent, and transformational initiatives but also implement tools and capabilities to manage those various initiatives as part of an integrated whole.

Eric Schmidt's Journey to Codify the 70-20-10 Formula

If you invested in Google's IPO in August 2004, you're probably feeling pretty good. As of July 2018, Google's (Alphabet) stock price has risen almost 2,300 percent since the IPO. And one of the key drivers has been its enviable continuous transformation record thanks to the efforts of then CEO Eric Schmidt's effort to codify constant transformation.

Eric Emerson Schmidt was born in Virginia to Eleanor and Wilson Schmidt. He was one of three kids in a highly educated family. After initial education on the East Coast, Schmidt found himself at UC Berkeley for his masters and PhD. Schmidt followed an IT career in several illustrious organizations, including Bell Labs, Xerox PARC, and Sun Microsystems. In 1997, he was appointed CEO and chairman of the board at Novell. In 2001, Google founders Larry Page and Sergey

Brin were looking to hire someone to run the company and chose Schmidt. He was asked to build the corporate infrastructure needed for a fast-growing company.

Schmidt quickly realized that the best way to win consistently in a fast-changing world was to hire the best people and to create an environment that actively fertilized their creativity. Innovation wasn't just the job of a few people working in lab coats and bunkers. In the most innovative organizations, innovation was a verb, not a noun.

Schmidt hit upon the idea of using the 70-20-10 model to fuel constant growth in the current business as well as to discover new businesses. This sounds good in concept, but Google's first challenge was how to put this into practice. In an interview with *Business 2.0* magazine, Schmidt said, "For a while we put the projects in different rooms. That way, if we were in one room too long, we knew we were not spending our time correctly. It was sort of a stupid device, but it worked quite well. Now we have people who actually manage this, so I know how I spend my time, and I do spend it 70-20-10."

During Schmidt's days at Google, 70 percent activities included areas like core search and ads. The 20 percent adjacencies were products such as Google News, Google Earth, and Google Local. And an example of the 10 percent activities included the Wi-Fi initiative aimed at broad access at no cost to connect more people to the internet in the early 2000s.

The 70-20-10 model continues to be used, with some variations in the numbers, by a large number of highly innovative companies. The risk-managed portfolio effect of mixing big-bet projects with incremental-bet efforts is undeniable.

How to Focus on the 10 in the 70-20-10 Model

Executing innovations in the 70 and 20 parts of the 70-20-10 model is well understood. It's the disruptive innovation work (i.e., the 10 in the 70-20-10) that requires a very different mindset and therefore new discipline. This is where the concept, popularized by Alphabet—moonshot thinking—is useful. The term "moonshot thinking" comes from the original challenge from President John F. Kennedy to go to the moon. It advocates for ideas that deliver ten times the impact (10X) instead of incremental ones. The Alphabet company X (previously called Google X) is the main proponent of this type of thinking. X has claimed that sometimes it is easier to make something ten times better than to improve it 10 percent. While that may be controversial, the point is that going after a 10X improvement demands breaking all existing paradigms about the problem. Anything else leads to incremental thinking. Thus, 10X is a great framework to separate incremental thinking from disruptive thinking. The rewards for getting a disruptive idea right can be huge. For instance, Alphabet/Google's driverless car company, Waymo, has been valued at over $100 billion by UBS.

Setting Up a 10X Disruption (Moonshot) Factory

Google's approach to 10X has been to create a separate edge organization, X, previously known as Google X. It's a good study of generating large numbers of ideas and then running a select number through a disciplined portfolio.

Alphabet generates hundreds of intrapreneurship ideas internally and in addition sources thousands more from its conferences and crowdsourcing activities. Of these, only a small fraction makes it to the 10X processing factory that is X.

X is set up to run a portfolio of 10X projects only. Alphabet's other businesses focus on their routine operations (the 70 in 70-20-10) and continuous improvements (the 20).

The winnowing down from the thousands of potential ideas into the small portfolio of 10X projects is done via a combination of hard data and the judgment of the top scientists at X who ultimately decide on the fate of the ideas. Even after the ideas get selected to become the few chosen projects, they are run iteratively to kill off as many low-value ideas as early in the cycle as possible. What remains after the constant winnowing is a small set of highly disruptive projects. Among these, X lists big-hitter ideas like Google Brain (which powers speech recognition, photo search, and video recommendations), Google Contact Lens (which assists diabetics by monitoring glucose levels), and self-driving cars, and has other exciting products in Project Loon (providing internet access via balloons in the stratosphere), Project Wing (delivering products across a city using flying vehicles), and Project Glass (delivering augmented reality via a head-mounted display).

> Remarkably, many digital transformations skip over the opportunity to run a 10X disruptive portfolio because they assume it is too upstream or too expensive. Nothing could be further from the truth. The Next Generation Services program spent little to no money, focused exclusively on 10X ideas, and paid off in less than two years.

The Volume Part of Strategy Sufficiency

A good portfolio mix in your personal financial investment plan helps optimize risk. However, whether the plan generates enough returns for you to, say, retire comfortably depends on how much you invest into the plan. This "volume of input" has a parallel in digital transformation as well, i.e., how many ideas and projects are being funneled into the transformation effort. The systemic generation of enough transformation *projects* (i.e., beyond generating *ideas*) is foundational to generating enough fuel for sufficient transformation. There are many approaches to generating these ideas for projects, but the one that I like the most, because it also helps change the culture of the entire organization, is "intrapreneurship," a system for employing the practices of entrepreneurship within a large organization.

Targeted intrapreneurship can generate enough transformation projects (i.e., fuel) for sufficient transformation.

To be clear, intrapreneurship without the rest of the disciplines of digital transformation produces little fruit. However, when supported by the rest of the disciplines of digital transformation, it is a powerful tool. Many well-known iconic products have come from intrapreneurship programs within some of the world's leading companies, including:

- DLP (Digital Light Processing) technology—Texas Instruments
- Elixir guitar strings—W. L. Gore
- Gmail—Google
- Post-it Notes—3M
- Java programming language—Sun Microsystems

- PlayStation—Sony

- in-store health clinics—Walmart

- several movie scripts—DreamWorks

But the example of intrapreneurship that I find most striking is Virgin Group. Sir Richard Branson, the founder of Virgin Group, is a strong proponent of disciplined transformation led via intrapreneurship.

The Virgin Group's Approach to Intrapreneurship

By most objective metrics, Sir Richard Branson has been a highly successful serial entrepreneur. His Virgin Group has spawned more than five hundred companies and currently holds more than two hundred. For a group that has been in existence less than five decades, that's a remarkable record.

It is the sheer breadth of industries in the holding and the success rates in business that is fascinating. How does the Virgin Group drive consistency across such varied businesses? In an article for *Entrepreneur* magazine, Branson talked about the importance of intrapreneurship in driving perpetual transformation in the group. "What if CEO stood for 'chief enabling officer'? What if that CEO's primary role were to nurture a breed of intrapreneurs who would grow into tomorrow's entrepreneurs?" Branson admits that Virgin has stumbled onto this model because when they entered businesses in which they had very little knowledge, they had to enable a few select people who knew what they were doing. The intrapreneurship model has clearly paid off for Virgin.

Virgin's processes are highly conducive to intrapreneurship, with disciplined communications, training, and ideation processes designed to generate internal ideas. Several of Virgin's innovations, including the herringbone design of business-class seats in commercial airliners that give each flyer a sleeper aisle seat, owe their existence to Virgin's intrapreneurship program (see sidebar). The Virgin Group's culture mirrors the style of its founder. Branson is a known enabler who firmly believes in empowering his people to make decisions. He has some fundamental business principles, one of them being to protect the downside. Another principle is to have fun in your business. Branson uses this as a criterion for choosing which businesses to enter. The disciplined processes to gather innovations based on these principles bottom-up, and then mash them up with top-down strategy, serves as a powerful source of constant change at Virgin[32,33,34] as demonstrated by their innovation record.

There's another side benefit of the intrapreneurial culture of Virgin. It also serves to propagate a culture of ongoing change acceptance. I will return to this point in chapter 11, "Agile Culture."

Sir Richard Branson's Journey to Create an Ever-Evolving Giant . . . and His Love of Intrapreneurship

Richard Charles Nicholas Branson was born in Surrey, England, in 1950 to a barrister and a flight attendant. Branson struggled in early life with dyslexia, having a hard time with traditional schooling institutions. At the age of sixteen, he convinced his father to let him drop out of his boarding school in Stowe, England, to start a magazine called *Student*. His dad agreed, but only on the condition that he sell £4,000 in advertising to cover his costs. Branson ended up selling £8,000 of advertising and distributed fifty thousand copies of the magazine for free.

In 1969, Branson came up with the idea of starting a mail-order record company to fund his magazine. Branson and his business partner, Nik Powell, considered themselves as virgins in business and chose that name for their enterprise. That experience led to the opening of a record shop and then eventually a recording studio in Oxfordshire. The big business breakthrough came with Virgin Records. Their first artist, Mike Oldfield, recorded a huge hit song, "Tubular Bells," which led Virgin Records to sign up iconic artists like the Rolling Stones, Culture Club, and Genesis over time.

In 1980, Branson branched out into the travel business, starting up the Voyager Group, followed by Virgin Atlantic in 1984. The Virgin Group was formally incorporated in 1989 as a holding group. Virgin's businesses have ranged from travel (Virgin Atlantic) to health (Virgin Health Bank) to books (Virgin Books) to aerospace (Virgin Galactic), with net revenues of £19.5 billion (2016).

Branson has consistently been a strong evangelist of intrapreneurship. He credits it for several innovations within Virgin. Speaking on a few memorable examples, he says, "One example that springs to mind was at Virgin Atlantic, about ten years ago. None of the big expensive seat design firms seemed able to solve the design problems posed by our specifications for our upper-class cabin, but a young designer, Joe Ferry, volunteered (insistently) to give the project a go. We set him loose, and the herringbone-configured private sleeper suites that resulted from his 'outside the box' creativity put us years ahead of the pack and made for millions of very happy horizontal fliers."

Strategy Sufficiency at Procter & Gamble's NGS

One of the lessons learned from past attempts to set up innovation in GBS was that having a handful of big-hitter ideas doesn't make for a disciplined and sufficient portfolio of outcomes. Therefore, we needed to address both the "right mix" and the "right volume" issues for sustainable transformation. We looked at various options and eventually set up NGS to focus only on 10X disruptive change experiments (projects), while the core organization would drive continuous improvements, i.e., the 70 and the 20 in the 70-20-10 model. Recognizing that 10X disruptions require different processes and reward systems than those in normal operations, this split made sense. It allowed us to implement different designs for rewards, recognition, and risk management in NGS that would be different from the rest of the company.

For instance, one example of how we cultivated and supported high-risk, high-return projects was by creating new terminology. The term "projects" was replaced by "experiments." Projects come with an expectation of success, whereas experiments convey a riskier proposition to the core organization.

Another example of a process to cultivate moonshot behavior was the composition of the NGS portfolio itself. We came up with the strategy of 10-5-4-1, which I mentioned previously. That ratio was based on what some venture capitalists do within their portfolios, and it worked for NGS too.

The volume part of strategy sufficiency was addressed by leveraging our vast ecosystem of internal and external resources to generate hundreds of ideas. Put together, the way NGS's strategy sufficiency worked was simple—the internal and external ecosystems generated a large number of ideas (which were always in response to a strategic GBS opportunity area). Of these, in a given year we might pick ten to turn into formal experiments. And then the 10-5-4-1 ratio was applied in execution.

Chapter Summary

- For sufficient digital transformation, it's important to distinguish between anecdotal success stories and systemic transformation. A sustainable digital transformation draws on a large number of innovation ideas and then processes them efficiently to kill most of them. Strategy sufficiency therefore includes the ability to generate sufficiency in terms of numbers of ideas as well as the portfolio sufficiency to turn some of them into major successes.

- Running effective portfolios such as the 70-20-10 model can help in making digital transformation plans sustainable.

- Within the 70-20-10 mix, moonshot thinking, or the 10X approach, is a powerful tool to generate ideas for the 10 segment.

- Intrapreneurship programs are a great mechanism to generate sufficient numbers of ideas.

Your Disciplines Checklist

Evaluate your digital transformation against the questions in figure 18 to follow a disciplined approach to each step in Digital Transformation 5.0.

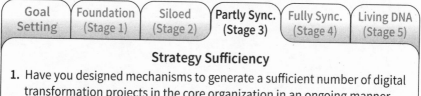

| Goal Setting | Foundation (Stage 1) | Siloed (Stage 2) | Partly Sync. (Stage 3) | Fully Sync. (Stage 4) | Living DNA (Stage 5) |

Strategy Sufficiency

1. Have you designed mechanisms to generate a sufficient number of digital transformation projects in the core organization in an ongoing manner (intrapreneurship)?

2. Do you have a mechanism that will allow you to take a select number of big, disruptive ideas from the pilot tests and scale them up rapidly?

3. Do you have mechanisms, including risk/reward systems, that allow for at least 50 percent of your initiatives to fail forward?

4. Have you separated resources and success criteria between the 70 (core operational activities), the 20 (continuous improvement activities of the core) and the 10 (disruptive innovation)?

5. Have you identified the right metrics for success, in order to celebrate digital transformation outcomes, not just corporate innovation theater activities?

Figure 18 Your disciplines checklist for strategy sufficiency

Stage 4

Fully Synchronized

What Is Stage 4?	The point where an enterprise-wide digital platform or new business model has fully taken root. However, it is a one-time transformation. It is still just one technology (or business model) change away from being disrupted
Causes of Failure	Inability to complete the one-time digital transformation due to either organization structure issues or digital literacy issues.
Disciplines to Address Risks	<ul><li>*Digital reorganization* to reboot technical capabilities both in the IT function and the rest of the enterprise.</li><li>*Staying current* on the rapidly evolving technology landscape, both for completion of the one-time transformation and its successful ongoing operation.</li></ul>

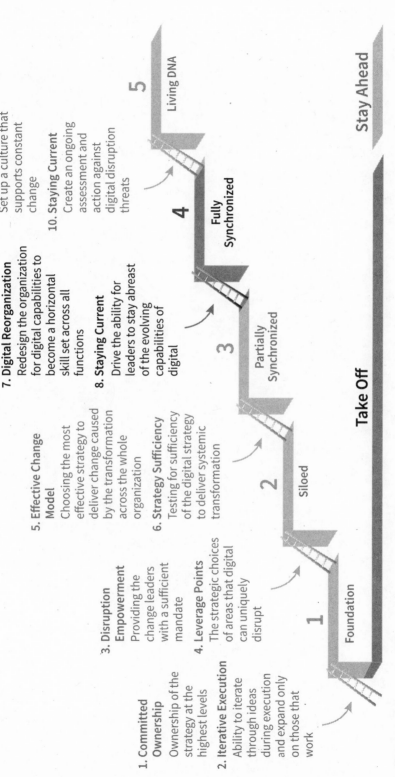

Figure 19 Stage 4 digital transformation disciplines

1. Committed Ownership
Ownership of the strategy at the highest levels

2. Iterative Execution
Ability to iterate through ideas during execution and expand only on those that work

3. Disruption Empowerment
Providing the change leaders with a sufficient mandate

4. Leverage Points
The strategic choices of areas that digital can uniquely disrupt

5. Effective Change Model
Choosing the most effective strategy to deliver change caused by the transformation across the whole organization

6. Strategy Sufficiency
Testing for sufficiency of the digital strategy to deliver systemic transformation

7. Digital Reorganization
Redesign the organization for digital capabilities to become a horizontal skill set across all functions

8. Staying Current
Drive the ability for leaders to stay abreast of the evolving capabilities of digital

9. Agile Culture
Set up a culture that supports constant change

10. Staying Current
Create an ongoing assessment and action against digital disruption threats

5 Living DNA

4 Fully Synchronized

3 Partially Synchronized

2 Siloed

1 Foundation

Stay Ahead

Take Off

Chapter 9

Digital Reorganization

Imagine attaching a World War II airplane engine to a modern commercial jet aircraft. You don't have to be an aeronautical engineer to know that this would be an unviable design. The old engine would not have the power needed for the plane to take off and stay aloft. And yet, most enterprises undergoing digital transformation do exactly that when they rely on older versions of IT organization structures and capabilities to power the change! This can be fatal to attaining a fully synchronized Stage 4 digital transformation.

The digital enterprise needs a new design of engine (i.e., IT function) to power takeoff and staying aloft, just as modern aircraft needed a new breed of engines in the 1940s. The modern engines for digital are the new IT function capabilities. Additionally, the aircraft itself will need to be constructed of modern materials, which I use as an analogy for the need to upgrade digital literacy broadly across the enterprise.

I'll start with the first topic, the need for a newer design of engine. Once again, the aircraft analogy helps here. Early aircraft designs were based on piston engines, like the ones that power lawn mowers today. Airplanes were light, they carried a limited number of passengers, and they flew mostly at relatively low altitudes in nonpressurized cabins. By the 1940s, the need for military-grade aircraft that demanded higher speeds drove the industry to develop more powerful piston engines. The evolution from simpler aircraft design to heavier, faster, better-performing jets necessitated a different design of engine altogether. To facilitate this transformation, aircraft designs started to move to gas-turbine engines.

As businesses evolve to a digitally transformed state in the Fourth Industrial Revolution, a similar question arises with the IT organization's capabilities. Are you powering your digital transformation with a piston-engine IT function or a gas-turbine one?

The Evolution of Aircraft Engines from the Time of the Wright Brothers to Now

In 1903, the Wright brothers wanted to source an engine for their new airplane. They sent out requests for proposals for an engine that would produce at least 8 horsepower (HP) and would weigh no more than 200 pounds. They got no response. Having had some experience in this arena, they decided to build it themselves. And so, the first Wright engine was built; it produced all of 12 HP! It ran on gas, had four cylinders, was made of aluminum, and weighed 170 pounds. Fast-forward a century, and aircraft engines have evolved significantly. They are much more powerful, for one. In contrast to the 12 HP Wright engine, a typical engine on a Boeing 737-500 produces roughly 18,000 HP. Even the smallest Honda Civic is thirteen times more powerful than the first Wright engine!

Meanwhile, the gas-powered piston engine design, like the one used by the Wright brothers, continued to power aircraft for the next four decades, but it eventually had to confront limitations in its design for modern aircraft. It wasn't until the late 1930s to early 1940s that production engine design ventured from pistons to gas turbines, based on a design patented by Sir Frank Whittle.

Gas-turbine engines would offer the next generation of capabilities. They inherently operate on totally different mechanical principles. Piston engines are essentially based on a reciprocating mechanism (to-and-fro motion) that converts energy from a combustion process into a mechanical motion.

In contrast, gas turbines have no reciprocating parts but only rotating parts. They have rotating blades in the front of the engine that compress air, which is then mixed with fuel and combusted. It is the expanding gas produced from the combustion that is then forced through a small outlet that produces the thrust. That design delivered the next step-change in the power-to-weight ratio. Most commercial jets use them today, although smaller aircraft still tend to use piston engines.

The analogy of using new IT capabilities and skills as "engines" to power digital transformation is not without precedent. In organization design, people have long been considered as "change engines" of enterprises. Digital technology is considered as a "growth engine" for most organizations to increase revenue. Systemically putting together people and digital capabilities as transformation engines is a simple offshoot.

Is Your IT Function a Piston Engine or a Gas-Turbine Engine?

Before I launch into my engine analogy, we need to take a brief detour into terminology. Different enterprises have different names for the organizations involved in digital capabilities, e.g., IT function, Chief Digital Officer function, Global Business Services, or Transformation Office. Currently, most enterprises also have multiple organizations doing these functions. I strongly believe that all these enabling digital functions eventually need to come together. That is a major part of the "engine upgrade" covered in this chapter. Meanwhile, these multiple organizations have left us with a dilemma on what to call this collective group. For reasons of simplicity, I refer to all of them collectively as the "IT function" in this chapter.

As we've learned from the experience of constantly upgrading our smartphones, technology gets old fast. That's true of IT functions in the enterprise as well. IT technologies, IT scope of operations, and IT skills all have incredibly short life cycles. That's been historically true and is not a surprise. What's new is that the piston-engine version of IT has reached an inflection point. It needs a consciously different engine. We're no longer talking evolution; we're talking about a dramatically different redesign. The new IT function is not just about new technology platforms, a new charter of work, or newer skills; it is about leading all the other functions and business units in the company to new technology-enabled business models. The digital enterprise needs digital to be done by every function, but powered by IT. Which is why I believe that the new IT function needs a totally new charter and a new name—the digital resources function.

The piston-engine version of IT has reached an inflection point. It needs a consciously different engine, a totally new charter, and a new name—the digital resources function.

The Discipline of Redesigning for the Next Generation of IT Capabilities

To understand why a new IT function "engine" is needed, it might help to start with its role. The historical role of IT has been as an enabler. It provided the automation for enterprise processes and functions such as finance, sales, marketing, manufacturing, HR, and others to be efficient. That continues to be the bread-and-butter work in most IT organizations (see figure 20).

Meanwhile, over the past fifteen years, a new breed of businesses started to evolve—digitally native companies. The digitally native companies didn't just think of IT as an enabling function; they based their entire business on data and digital technology. So, whereas Barnes & Noble started with physical stores and books, Amazon started with a website that took orders and payments and then built their physical processes later. Technology wasn't just an enabler, it was the entire foundation of their business model.

Initially, the incumbent companies weren't too concerned. They believed that these digital natives didn't have the partnerships, physical presence, resources, or operational skills to be a real threat. With time, this has turned out to be a fallacy. Digitally native companies have the advantage of speed (e.g., online airline booking vs. old travel agencies) and the possibility of creating entirely new digital business models (e.g., Airbnb crowdsourcing its room space). In other words, IT technology has gone from being an enabler in the old enterprises to being the only

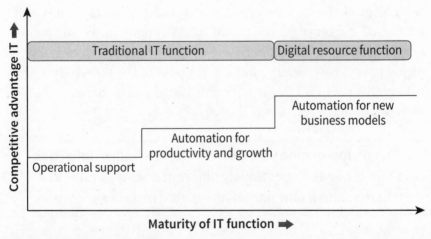

Figure 20 IT function maturity

way in which digitally native companies operate. Along with this new role of IT, there needs to be a rebirth of the IT function itself.

Building a New Generation of IT Capabilities via the Digital Resources Function

At its heart is the change from "managing" technology to "leading" the digital ecosystem of the enterprise. The change isn't just administrative, though; there are technologies, platforms, and people skills that will need to be redone. I have identified six vectors of change:

- *More flexible technology platforms*: Amazon and other digitally native companies have the capability to make hundreds of noticeable changes to their systems to test out new business models *daily*. They use a new generation of digital capabilities to blend scale with speed to support constantly evolving digital business models. In contrast, the current technologies in most enterprises were originally built for enterprise efficiency and scale. They are large and complex, took a long time to implement, and take even longer to modify. Think large enterprise resource planning (e.g., SAP) implementations. These monolithic systems worked extremely well in the past because the goal at the time was scale. The new digital revolution has changed that goal.

- *More agility in execution*: Ask any large enterprise business unit leader their opinion on IT projects in general and you will likely find their response liberally sprinkled with "millions of dollars" and "years to implement." Meanwhile, a digitally native start-up could rent a server with order-processing software and have a business up and running in minutes. Large enterprise IT organizations have a big challenge with agile execution.

- *Skills on newer technology*: The top five high-paying skills of 2018 according to *CIO* magazine[35] are information security, DevOps, data science, business application development, and machine learning. The only thing you need to know as a leader in the Fourth Industrial Revolution is that perhaps only one of these five—business application development—would have been on that list five years ago. How many of your IT professionals have been in the enterprise for more than five years? How many have kept up with the latest skills?

- *New capabilities to lead digital transformation*: The IT professional of the future will need as many nontechnical skills—including creativity, communications, influencing, and teamwork—as technical. Further, I use the term "technical" in its broadest sense to include items such as process mapping, business model design, and lean execution, in addition to IT technology. This is to be expected as the role of the IT function evolves from "doing" technology to "leading" digital transformation. The new digital resources function requires a skill set that is of a transformational leader who also happens to be a guru on technology. The traditional approach has been to rely on consultancies that seem to have such a mix. There may be a legitimate role, especially during transition, for consultancies. However, this is problematic long-term, keeping in mind the goal of leading perpetual Stage 5 transformation as I will cover in the next stage.

- *Governance of the digital ecosystem*: The freelance workforce in the US is growing three times faster than the overall workforce and is projected to be the majority by 2027.[36] Within the freelance workforce, the growth in IT is faster than most other functions. Also, as systems across one enterprise to another become more interconnected, the predominant skill set in demand will become more governing and less managing.

- *Updated vendor ecosystem*: It's very likely that the mix of IT vendors and partners who were associated with the old IT function may not be the best fit for the digital resources function. Part of this is easy to understand—the vendors who were optimal for stability and cost-efficiency goals might not be fit for digital transformation. However, that's only half the issue. The other half is that the same digital disruptive forces are acting upon the IT industry as well. Traditional IT service partners are being squeezed as their people-centric businesses get disrupted. Being locked into multimillion-dollar, multiyear contracts with the older-generation IT providers, even for "commodity IT" services, may not be in your best interests. Current contracts may be optimized for cost efficiency over agility and innovation. The dirty little secret of IT outsourcing is that the IT providers take a given scope of work, freeze it, and promise to deliver it for 15 to 50 percent less cost partly by ruthlessly optimizing efficiencies and partly because there's not much innovation on the old scope of work.

Upgrading the digital resources function "engine" is only half the job. The rest is to complement it with a new "airplane design" of enterprise-wide digital capabilities, as covered in the next section.

What Does the Digital Resources Function Look Like?

It looks like an octopus: A central brain, but decentralized presence. A thin layer for a few controls (e.g., info security, data standards, and high-level open architecture), along with roles for digital capability building and disruptive innovation. This is the end-state structure, and it's almost certain that the structure will be much larger during the digital transformation itself than at the end state.

Within the IT organization itself, the skills will include a mix of "left brain" and "right brain." Soft skills to manage via influence and hard skills on governance. Creativity to keep generating new business models and technical skills to execute them. Disciplines such as user experience, design thinking, strategic disruptive innovation, or process-systems thinking will be as important as hard-core technology or industry vertical skills.

Is the Name Change Necessary?

The new name itself provides an important sign of intent. This is a shift from a technology focus to a resource focus. This is also an opportunity to set a clear direction of Stage 5 perpetual digital transformation. More tactically, this can also bring some sanity to the confusing array of titles that have suddenly sprung up, e.g., Chief Digital Officer, Chief Data Officer, Chief Analytics Officer, Transformation Officer, Chief Information Security Officer, Chief Information Officer, and Global Business Services Officer.

Building New Enterprise-Wide Digital Human Capabilities

In 2014, AT&T started an ambitious effort to retrain 100,000 people in its workforce to get ready for a digitally enabled future. Of the company's 250,000-strong workforce, about half worked in science, technology, engineering, and math fields. Roughly 100,000 worked in hardware functions that would not exist in the next decade.[37] The choices were not easy—hire tens of thousands of people skilled in new technologies or invest significantly in retraining the existing workforce.

AT&T chose the latter. Today, its Workforce2020 program plans to spend a billion dollars on a web-based multiyear effort that includes partnerships with universities and online course providers as well as new internal capabilities for career development for the future.

The strategy is a bold one that has a sound basis. New digital technology skills in fields such as AI, cloud computing, and cybersecurity are not just in short supply but are also evolving faster than you can hire new people.[38] Traditional hiring and training programs cannot keep up. The alternative approach is to re-skill the existing workforce to address at least part of the gap.

Enterprise-wide digital re-skilling builds the critical human resource capabilities necessary to operate the new digital backbone of enterprise.

A Stage 5 digital transformation involves embedding digital capabilities into the very fiber of the enterprise. It's a major strategic choice that requires new human resource capabilities to operate the new digital backbone of enterprise. Retraining the mass of the current workforce is one of the major choices possible. However, the effort of developing a new digital backbone of the enterprise (i.e., where technology is not just an enabler but is the entire foundation of the business model itself) will need more than employee retraining. Here's the total list:

- *Re-skilling the entire workforce*: Is there a deliberate HR transformation plan to create the digital workforce of the future?

- *Re-skilling the leadership*: Do we have sufficiency of skills at the top leadership level to truly leverage digital? In private enterprises, this starts at the board level.

- *New human/machine interface policies*: Have we created new guidelines and policies on where and how humans and machines will coexist?

- *New security protocols*: Do we have sufficient capabilities in personal and proprietary information security in the digital world—including both policies and technology?

- *Fluid organization structures*: What's the organizing model in the post-functions world? How should the workforce organize around tasks as opposed to rigid functional boundaries? This starts with the organizing model of the digital resources function.

Together, the restructured IT function and the re-skilled digital capabilities in the enterprise provide the opportunity for the new digital capabilities and tools to take root. They provide the redesigned complete "airplane" for the Fourth Industrial Revolution.

Chapter Summary

- Stage 4 transformations fail because the digital operation does not take root. This is primarily a human capability and re-skilling challenge.

- Addressing this human re-skilling has two parts. First is building a new IT function, which I call the "digital resources function," which plays the role of enabling, governance, and ongoing facilitation of digital innovation. The second is the digital re-skilling of the rest of the enterprise.

- The digital resources function structure must address the agility of digital systems and processes, the retraining of IT experts on newer technology and processes, and rebuilding the vendor ecosystem for the new economy.

- The enterprise-wide digital re-skilling should attack the issues of digital literacy across the board, policies for human/machine interface, digital security, and fluid organization structures.

Your Disciplines Checklist

Evaluate your digital transformation against the questions in figure 21 to follow a disciplined approach to each step in Digital Transformation 5.0.

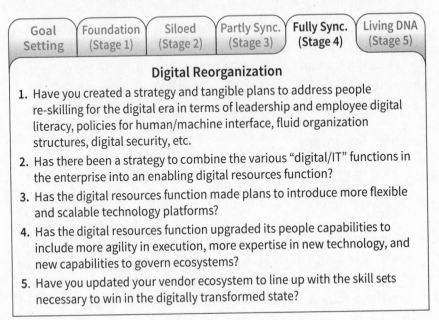

| Goal Setting | Foundation (Stage 1) | Siloed (Stage 2) | Partly Sync. (Stage 3) | **Fully Sync. (Stage 4)** | Living DNA (Stage 5) |

Digital Reorganization

1. Have you created a strategy and tangible plans to address people re-skilling for the digital era in terms of leadership and employee digital literacy, policies for human/machine interface, fluid organization structures, digital security, etc.

2. Has there been a strategy to combine the various "digital/IT" functions in the enterprise into an enabling digital resources function?

3. Has the digital resources function made plans to introduce more flexible and scalable technology platforms?

4. Has the digital resources function upgraded its people capabilities to include more agility in execution, more expertise in new technology, and new capabilities to govern ecosystems?

5. Have you updated your vendor ecosystem to line up with the skill sets necessary to win in the digitally transformed state?

Figure 21 Your disciplines checklist for digital reorganization

Chapter 10

Staying Current

"Where could we use blockchain at P&G?" I recall asking a couple of smart start-up founders in June 2015. We were at their Silicon Valley offices, which had glass conference rooms hung from the ceiling over an atrium. It looked as futuristic as blockchain technology, which is essentially a secure chain of data blocks, each connected to the one before it, fully verified and managed without a central authority. It's fascinating because it is considered to be unhackable. It has the ability to correctly and securely log any transaction, thus eliminating processes such as validation and reconciliation. That's relevant since most operations in any enterprise are done as transactions—whether placing an order or paying for it. If transactions could be made accurate and secure from their earliest source to their last destination (for example, from sourcing potatoes in Peru to selling chips in the UK), that would certainly disrupt the way enterprises ran their operations.

The brainstorming that followed my question was intellectually stimulating but unsatisfying. Uses could include tracking discount coupons, advertising, creating a P&G cryptocurrency to ease intra-company transactions and sales across countries, and so on. The problem was, none of these were available as solutions even in their basic forms. The current products of the start-up were all aimed at the average consumer (e.g., how to pay for coffee at the store). I left the meeting having mentally filed away blockchain as a powerful technology that was not ripe for primetime in the enterprise.

Six months later, I ran across the same start-up. Their current product offerings included several enterprise-related blockchain solutions, including tracking international shipping from corporate suppliers, highly secure financial accounting, and anti-counterfeiting certification of consumer products. Although I was delighted at the progress, it also left me slightly disheartened. If I, in my transformation leader role, found it hard to stay current with the pace of change in technology, then how would the average operational leader cope?

Staying Current in a Volatile Digital World

Keeping track of all the sources of disruption and the exciting possibilities in a digital world can seem like an impossible task. That's true for us in our role as consumers as it is in our professional lives as, say, entrepreneurs/executives/public sector leaders. The explosive growth of capabilities in digital technology is mind-boggling. A teenager has more computing power available on his or her smartphone today than President Bill Clinton had at his disposal while in office. They can make phone calls for free to Asia or Africa over WhatsApp—calls that used to cost $3 per minute thirty years ago.

In our lives as consumers, we see real-time financial and sports updates posted on Yahoo. Each of these is a short, similar-sounding paragraph. That makes total sense, since 90 percent of them are written by robots. I read tweets from the police in my city of Cincinnati that say, "Shooting in Avondale tonight, victim lied about where it occurred until confronted with @shotspotter evidence! @CinciPD." ShotSpotter is the acoustic triangulation technology used in London, New York, and other cities that use analytics to accurately pinpoint where shots are fired and directs the police to these locations in real time.

As a business executive, I see large tech-savvy customers make accounts receivables claims that can number in the thousands *for each order*—each claim being worth as little as a few cents. Clearly, these are being generated by robots. It wouldn't be cost-effective for a human to create these micro-transactions worth a few cents each.

In our NGS scouting trips for solutions for P&G, I saw AI that could replace experienced lawyers on highly personalized contract negotiations and robotic products originally created for defense applications that could rival Robocop. There were automated meeting rooms that could recognize you as you entered and start up the upcoming videoconference meeting on your calendar without a single click. I saw solutions that could make the whole chore of creating travel expense reports an archaic practice from the past and real-time language translation capabilities that could beat experienced humans. It can seem a bit overwhelming to an executive who needs to understand what's possible first and then decide where to focus.

Insights on Where to Stay Current

It's obviously a waste of time and effort to try and be on top of every new digital development. Through my work over the years, I have realized that there are some principles that can help us stay current in a focused manner. This applies equally to staying current on knowledge as well as on using disruptive product capabilities.

- *Track possible disruptions, but invest only in applied innovation*: At P&G, I first came across picture-taking technology to recognize products on retail store shelves in 2007 that could quickly tell manufacturers if their products were out of stock or incorrectly shelved. It was an interesting concept that was not ready for application. We checked it out every year after that until it suddenly became sufficiently mature for use in 2010. After that, we moved rapidly to deploy.

- *Take the slow train that's here instead of a fast train that might come later*: This was an interesting analogy that arose during a conversation with Salim Ismail. On disruptive technology, it's usually better to jump onto a slow train that's here and working rather than wait on the promise of a faster train that might come later. It delivers benefits faster, since no solution is permanent anyway. In other words, don't wait to start experimenting if the current product is already viable, even if imperfect.

- *Go for quick "disposable" solutions that pay out quickly*: This is a corollary to the previous "slow train" principle. The risk of losing money with an imperfect disruptive solution is mitigated if it pays out in a year or two anyway.

These principles have helped me on assessing and selecting where to focus. However, there's still the question of *how* to stay pragmatically current. In the following section I propose a few ideas. Additionally, to help with a quick update on the current state, appendix B at the end of the book provides a basic primer on a few select exponential technologies that are most likely to be disruptive to enterprises. I call these the "Exponential Five," and they include artificial intelligence, blockchain, smart process automation, drones and robotics, and industry-specific special-function exponential technologies such as genome editing.

The Discipline of How to Stay Current on Digital Technologies

The discipline of how to stay pragmatically current is not time consuming and can be built into the day-to-day routine of leaders. Here are a few activities that can be woven into the processes of every enterprise. I have found these to be extremely effective.

- Creating executive learning opportunities

- Partnering with venture capitalists (VCs) and start-ups

- Leveraging partners for education

- Opening up your data via APIs (data gateways) to others

- Enlisting the help of digital ambassadors (tech-savvy users)

Let's break down each one.

Creating Executive Learning Opportunities

Throughout my P&G career, I blocked out time every month to meet experts on digital technologies. This was in addition to reading books and online articles. The actual tactics varied with my role but included a combination of the following:

- *Reverse mentoring*: During my NGS role, I was very fortunate to have some of the best industry experts from other companies assigned to our team. I found our conversations over lunch or happy hour to be the best learning opportunities of my career. An offshoot of this approach can be peer mentoring, where a more senior person from the IT organization or an external agency can do the same.

There's no better way to get the organization moving on staying current than by setting an example.

- *Defining disruptive problems*: Engaging more frequently on defining specific disruptive problems is another win-win method. In NGS, our informal open-office culture helped. All sorts of problems were discussed in the open forum. Though I contributed my business experience into those discussions to help routine problem solving, I learned a tremendous amount about digital possibilities.

- *Adjacent or complementary industry pairing*: NGS set up an alliance of about ten large company shared services organizations, called the Shared Services Innovation Alliance, to share the most disruptive ideas across the group. We met every six months, and the small group discussions were priceless.

- *Organizing advisory resources*: Another effective mechanism is to organize advisory ecosystems on specific topics. The resources from Singularity University (SU) were particularly valuable here. I consider the bigger challenge of digital transformation to be change management, and here the SU network, including John Hagel III, was extremely helpful.

Partnering with Venture Capitalists and Start-Ups

Ninety percent of all the disruptive ideas that we worked on at NGS came from start-ups. This was true even though the NGS ecosystem included the world's best large digital companies. That's understandable, because disruption is what start-ups do. To tap into this, we set up a simple process. Every big GBS opportunity would promptly be summarized into a short paragraph and emailed to our venture capital partners. Our VCs were excellent in connecting us with start-ups working in that domain, and the subsequent dialogue produced very useful insights and business relationships.

There's a highly symbiotic relationship between VCs/start-ups and larger enterprises. VCs and start-ups need feedback from real "user" organizations, and enterprises need the latest thinking from them. Setting up periodic connections (e.g., a VC/start-up day) on-site at your organization (yes, they are willing to travel to you!) or organizing targeted visits to VC sites every six to twelve months would be a good start.

Setting up a periodic drumbeat of assigning your major partner companies a digital literacy slot in your organization can be beneficial to all organizations concerned.

Leveraging Partner Companies for Education

In the NGS team, we created a calendar of monthly slots on "hot technology" topics and offered both vendors and internal experts the opportunity to share knowledge in short bursts. Most partner companies are very eager to take advantage of free opportunities to bring in experts to client companies in the hope of establishing a strong equity of expertise. Setting up a periodic drumbeat of assigning your major partner companies a digital literacy slot in your organization can be beneficial to all organizations concerned.

Opening Up Your Data to Others Via Application Program Interfaces (APIs)

This is a highly innovative way to generate "applied" innovation and stay current at the same time. Here's how this works. Invite a targeted number of technical resources and software developers to access relevant data within your enterprise to either solve specific problems or even develop innovative uses based on it. Set up commercial agreements ahead of time to compensate and reward people for coming up with the most breakthrough ideas and apps. Access to data can be provided via secure APIs, which are gateway tools for others to either tap into specific data or talk to your programs. Once this competitive marketplace is set up, the creativity explodes. The capacity of the organization to attract and receive a large number of apps grows exponentially. Several large companies, including AT&T, Walmart, and FedEx, have created such API-based developer networks. At NGS, we created some crowdsourced prize-type opportunities using nonsensitive data even without creating an API portal.

Open up relevant data access via APIs to select internal and external developers and set up commercial models for them to benefit from the breakthrough apps they create.

Enlisting the Help of Digital Ambassadors (Tech-Savvy Users)

At P&G, we used our most tech-savvy users to occasionally train others or lead IT road shows in targeted areas. They loved the opportunity to be recognized for their IT expertise, and we were able to multiply the capacity of the IT function to quickly scale up operations using valuable experts.

Expert users from functions other than IT can be a great extension of your digital literacy army.

Chapter Summary

- Even the best digital transformation ideas can fail to take root in the organization that doesn't have the capability to best use them. In several cases, this is due to a lack of understanding of the digital capabilities. This is a tough problem because of the pace of change of digital technology.

- Certain principles for staying current on digital capabilities can help. These include the following:
  - ▸ Track possible disruptions, but invest only in applied innovation.
  - ▸ Take the slow train that's here instead of a fast train that might come later.
  - ▸ Go for quick "disposable" solutions that pay out quickly.

- There are disciplined ways to help the organization stay current on technology. This chapter offers five techniques.
  - ▸ Creating executive learning opportunities
  - ▸ Partnering with VCs and start-ups
  - ▸ Leveraging partners for education
  - ▸ Opening up your data via APIs to others
  - ▸ Enlisting the help of digital ambassadors (tech-savvy users)

- The technologies that are most likely to disrupt fall in the category of exponential technologies, i.e., technologies whose capabilities grow exponentially. Appendix B provides a quick primer on my pick of the most disruptive digital technologies. In summary they are:
  - ▸ *Artificial intelligence*: This is the most pervasive digital disruptive capability.
  - ▸ *Smart process automation*: This may be a low-hanging fruit for enterprise efficiency, but it also has significant capabilities to build agility of operations.
  - ▸ *Blockchain*: Its combination of decentralized transactions, easy access to many parties, and extremely high security has the ability to disrupt just about any transactional activity system.
  - ▸ *Robotics and drones*: Robotics and drones will disrupt any task that needs physical seeing, sensing, assisting, moving, measuring, or delivering—including those that need to be executed remotely.

▶ *Special-function technologies* (virtual reality, 3D printing, Internet of Things, nanotech, energy storage, biotechnology, advanced materials, etc.): Just about every industry has one or more of these that will disrupt its business model. The key is to identify and target the ones to invest in.

Your Disciplines Checklist

Evaluate your digital transformation against the questions in figure 22 to follow a disciplined approach to each step in Digital Transformation 5.0.

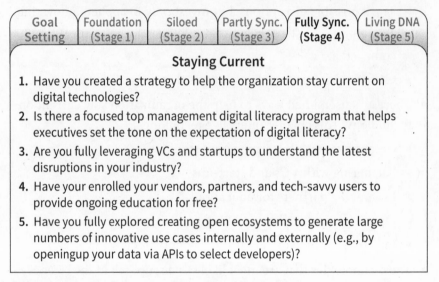

Goal Setting	Foundation (Stage 1)	Siloed (Stage 2)	Partly Sync. (Stage 3)	**Fully Sync. (Stage 4)**	Living DNA (Stage 5)

Staying Current

1. Have you created a strategy to help the organization stay current on digital technologies?
2. Is there a focused top management digital literacy program that helps executives set the tone on the expectation of digital literacy?
3. Are you fully leveraging VCs and startups to understand the latest disruptions in your industry?
4. Have your enrolled your vendors, partners, and tech-savvy users to provide ongoing education for free?
5. Have you fully explored creating open ecosystems to generate large numbers of innovative use cases internally and externally (e.g., by openingup your data via APIs to select developers)?

Figure 22 Your disciplines checklist for staying current

Stage 5

Living DNA

What Is Stage 5?	The stage of perpetual transformation. Constant reinvention and a highly agile culture become second nature to the organization. The enterprise becomes a disciplined market leader.
Causes of Failure	A loss of the edge that previously delivered a Stage 4 transformation, either due to an insufficiently agile culture or a lack of discipline to constantly sense and respond to new business disruption risks.
Disciplines to Address Risks	• *Agile culture* to support constant evolution of the business and organization. • *Sensing risk* to the enterprise routinely and reacting to them in a disciplined manner.

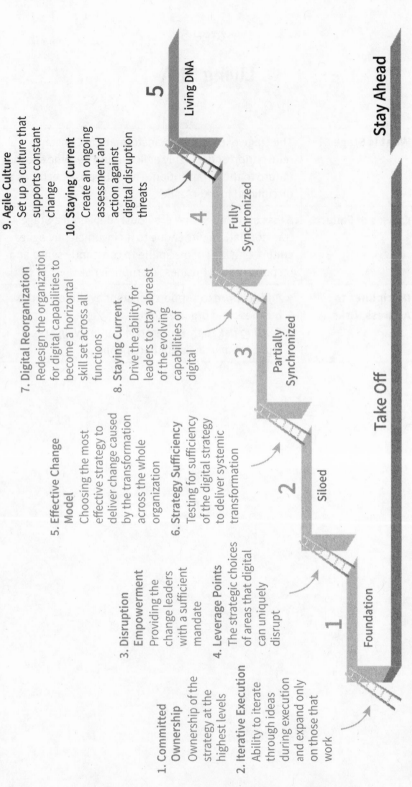

1. **Committed Ownership**
   Ownership of the strategy at the highest levels

2. **Iterative Execution**
   Ability to iterate through ideas during execution and expand only on those that work

3. **Disruption Empowerment**
   Providing the change leaders with a sufficient mandate

4. **Leverage Points**
   The strategic choices of areas that digital can uniquely disrupt

5. **Effective Change Model**
   Choosing the most effective strategy to deliver change caused by the transformation across the whole organization

6. **Strategy Sufficiency**
   Testing for sufficiency of the digital strategy to deliver systemic transformation

7. **Digital Reorganization**
   Redesign the organization for digital capabilities to become a horizontal skill set across all functions

8. **Staying Current**
   Drive the ability for leaders to stay abreast of the evolving capabilities of digital

9. **Agile Culture**
   Set up a culture that supports constant change

10. **Staying Current**
    Create an ongoing assessment and action against digital disruption threats

1 Foundation

2 Siloed

3 Partially Synchronized

4 Fully Synchronized

5 Living DNA

Take Off

Stay Ahead

Figure 23 Stage 5 digital transformation disciplines

Chapter 11

Agile Culture

The disruptions during an industrial revolution are constant. Uber, the original example of a digital disruptor, faces possible disruptions from driverless cars and local ride-sharing companies, not to mention flying taxis. That's where Stage 5 comes in as the state of staying ahead, or perpetual digital transformation.

The discipline of building an agile culture is a tried and tested approach to facilitate constant reinvention. Adobe, the global software company, is an excellent example of an enterprise that exhibits a constant state of reinvention. It started in the 1980s as a developer of PostScript printing software, moved on to graphics editing with Photoshop, and then built an enviable media and presentation software empire by the early 2000s. In 2013, it reinvented itself from being a digital media and marketing company that sold software packages to one that licensed the capabilities. That move revolutionized the way large software companies sold their products. It continues to evolve into new businesses in ecommerce today.

This business agility rests upon its enviable award-winning corporate culture, as I illustrate with the following example.

How Adobe's Agility Helps It Evolve Constantly

In 2012, an Adobe executive made a (well-intentioned) mistake[39] and ended up turning it into a big win for her company. According to *Forbes*,[40] in March 2012, Adobe's senior vice president for human resources, Donna Morris, was on a business trip to India. Despite having just arrived and still being a bit jet lagged, she agreed to an interview with an *Economic Times* reporter. The reporter asked her what she could do to disrupt HR. Morris, who felt strongly about how performance appraisals tend to hurt employee performance, spoke out: "We plan to abolish the annual performance review format." It was an excellent response, except for one minor detail—she had not talked about this idea yet with the Adobe CEO!

The next day the declaration was on the front page of the newspaper. Morris was aghast. She had to work furiously with the Adobe communications team to post an article on the company's intranet inviting employees to help assess and change Adobe's performance evaluation methods as soon as possible.

A culture that is welcoming of new ideas, even to the point of forgiving misplaced enthusiasm, will always evolve faster.

It all worked out perfectly in the end. A few months later, Adobe launched a new performance evaluation process. The formal annual reviews would be replaced by quarterly informal "check-ins." No paperwork was needed, although the discussions were expected to cover three things—expectations, feedback, and growth and development plans. Not surprisingly, the new process was received enthusiastically. And within two years of launch, Adobe had seen a 30 percent reduction in regretted attrition combined with a 50 percent increase in involuntary attrition of nonperformers. A culture that is welcoming of new ideas (even to the extent of forgiving misplaced enthusiasm) will have the agility to transform perpetually. Adobe has the ingredient of an agile culture necessary to help it transform constantly in the face of repeated disruptions.[41]

Adobe: Incentivizing Employees to Think Differently

Donna Morris's story isn't the only renowned example of Adobe's agile culture. Since 2013, Adobe's "Kickbox" innovation toolkit is often credited with driving a distinctive uptick in revenues and profits based on a field of employee-generated ideas. Here's how it works. You are given a literal box—a red cardboard box with everything you need to create and test an idea. The box comes with instructions, a pen, two Post-it pads, two notebooks, a bar of chocolate, a Starbucks gift card, and a $1,000 prepaid credit card. The instructions include a six-step process with checklists and exercises, with the final step being a management sell-in. The idea is to create an open innovation process where anyone can contribute ideas. In fact, the basic Kickbox is now available online for anyone to download.

The genius of the Kickbox idea isn't just the crowdsourcing of ideas; it's in the element of trusting and empowering its employees. Adobe risks $1,000 and employee time with each box. And yet as their innovation metrics have demonstrated, the return is well worth that risk.

Why Agile Culture Enables Perpetual Digital Transformation

An agile culture, not disruptive technology or new business models, is the ultimate disruption. Yes, I realize that sounds a bit trite, but once that statement is made actionable in the following paragraphs, I believe you'll agree that it's worth the risk of sounding trite.

The reason why comments about culture tend to be viewed as unhelpful is because culture is an outcome, not an action. In that context, any statement about culture is likely to be an unhelpful truism. However, based on my research of transformational companies that failed, I have identified that agile culture for perpetual digital transformation includes three sets of disciplined activities—customer-focused innovation, creating an adaptive environment, and establishing a shared common purpose. These provide the necessary outcome for success.

Agile culture in this context may be likened to air density for an airplane. The density of air directly drives the lift generated. At higher altitudes and at higher temperatures, planes work harder to generate lift. There exists a "flight ceiling," above which an airplane simply won't fly, because the lift generated would be insufficient for flight. Perpetual digital transformations generate a sufficiently agile culture (air density) to fly over traditional flight ceilings (constant disruptive trends).

The classic place to learn about innovative culture happens to be Silicon Valley. Not surprisingly, this is why corporate "tourism" to Silicon Valley has flourished. Initially, during the dot-com era, what some companies took away from the tours were the external trappings of freedom for their employees—the casual clothing and foosball tables. Over time, this has matured into reapplying entire processes and practices for ongoing innovation and agility. This includes lessons on the three items I mentioned before that, in combination, define an agile culture: customer-focused innovation, creating an adaptive environment, and fostering a shared purpose. To bring this to life, I'd like to use the following three case studies.

Agile culture for Stage 5 transformation = customer-focused innovation + adaptive environment + shared purpose

---

Zappos: How Customer-Focused Innovation Helps It Stay Ahead

Zappos is widely known for its customer-centric culture. Its dedication to customer service is legendary. Zappos was founded in 1999 under the domain name of ShoeSite.com. A few months later it changed its name to Zappos (based on the Spanish word for shoes, which is *zapatos*) to facilitate broadening its product range. Working in the highly personal-touch product area of shoe shopping, it defied all odds to hit $1 billion in sales in 2008. Zappos was acquired by Amazon in 2009.

Zappos: How Extreme Customer Focus Can Lead an Organization to Agility

In an interview with *Inc.* magazine in 2006, Zappos CEO and cofounder Tony Hsieh shared his fascinating journey that best articulates the cultural underpinnings of Zappos. In 1999, Hsieh and his colleague Alfred Lin received a call from a young entrepreneur, Nick Swinmurn, with an idea to sell shoes online. Hsieh was only twenty-four at the time, having just sold his company LinkExchange to Microsoft for about a quarter of a billion dollars. Hsieh says that he almost deleted Swinmurn's voice mail until he heard that the retail shoe market was $40 billion and growing 5 percent annually.

The challenge for the young founders was how to win online with what was essentially a physical experience–based product. They decided the answer would be to deliver the "absolutely best" service. Hsieh recalls that they agreed to an extraordinary vision of "we're a service company that just happens to sell shoes."

The Customer Is Boss

Cascading from that vision came customer-focused innovations that were sometimes risky. To deliver their service vision, they would need to control the whole customer experience. This meant dropping the model of having manufacturers shipping directly to customers and instead shipping the product from a Zappos warehouse—a decision that most supply chain efficiency consultants would balk at. They ran their warehouse 24/7 to deliver the fastest response to customers. Delivering the best service meant occasionally shopping for shoes with competitors, if that's what their customers needed. It meant free shipping as well as a 365-day no-questions-asked free returns policy. Hsieh preferred to invest money in improving customer service instead of advertising, betting on word of mouth to gain him long-term fans of the business.

Zappos's Amazing Customer Focus

Zappos's reps go the extra mile consistently. One story tells of a grieving person who was planning to return her shoes, but her mother had passed away recently and she didn't have the time. When Zappos emailed to enquire about the status of the return, the person shared what had happened. Zappos not only had the courier pick up the shoes at no extra cost but also sent her a large floral arrangement.

Zappos pioneered and perfected the art of turning personalized customer focus into a winning business model during the early days of online shopping, where online distribution channels struggled to be profitable. Zappos's fanatical focus on the customer is best exemplified by their distinctive call center service, where agents would go to any length to drive customer satisfaction. Call center agents have no limits on the time spent per call. In one instance recorded in December 2012, a Zappos customer service representative spent a whopping ten hours and twenty-nine minutes with a customer. What was even more remarkable was that the call wasn't about an order or even a complaint—it was about living in the Las Vegas area! In another example, Zappos earned a customer for life when the individual who was to be the best man at a wedding had his Zappos shoes misplaced by the courier. Zappos not only delivered a replacement overnight at no cost but also upgraded him to VIP status and gave him a full refund.

These examples are not anecdotal; they are the result of deliberate strategy. Zappos takes pains to recruit the right people, hire them mostly at entry level, and build them to be senior leaders within five to seven years. At the call centers, each recruit gets seven weeks of training before they get to the phones. Zappos was deliberate about neutralizing the no-physical-touch disadvantage of online shoe shopping via a business model that was incredibly customer-centric.

There's one final story that's worth sharing. Tony Hsieh repeats this frequently. After a night of bar hopping with clients, Hsieh and his clients found themselves back in the hotel room when one client happened to mention that they would have loved to get a pizza. The room service at the hotel was closed for the night. Hsieh suggested that they call the Zappos customer service line. The Zappos rep was initially taken aback but got back very quickly after a few minutes with the names of three nearby pizza shops that were open at that hour and helped place a delivery order for the pizza.[42]

A culture that puts the customer first will always be more receptive to accepting the changes needed to maintain customer service.

The best bet to keep an enterprise in sync with market disruptions is to foster rock-solid customer focus. To be clear, it doesn't need to underpin the entire business model, as with Zappos.[43] They initially chose customer-centricity to overcome the disadvantages of not having a physical store experience. What Zappos discovered along the way was that a culture that puts the customer first will always be more receptive to accepting changes needed to maintain customer service.

The next case study focuses on how an adaptive environment, or a lack of it, can affect innovation.

Adaptive Culture: Why the *New York Times*'s Initial Efforts on Digital Transformation Sputtered

In May 2014, an internal report on digital innovation at the venerable *New York Times* newspaper was leaked. It shared the struggles to adopt new ways of working driven by digital publishing, among other issues. The digital troops were airing their frustration with the gaps in people, processes, and systems that were necessary for the very future of the organization. These highlighted issues of a print-first culture that conflicted directly with the digital era.

For instance, many of the daily reporting and editorial activities were oriented toward finalizing the front page, called A1,[44] starting from a 10:00 a.m. meeting, to the early afternoon deadline for reporters to file summaries, to the verdict on which stories made it to the front page. All these activities were more suited to the rhythm of a traditional daily newspaper as opposed to real-time web-based news. The report also called out the need for new systems that were critical for a web-first future. The *Times* was behind on its data tagging and structuring. For example, it took the paper seven years to tag "September 11." The ability for its web readers to "follow" a certain topic was also subpar. All these were systems that were not very important in a print-first world but critical in a digital-first world.

Another issue highlighted was the ability to better understand readers' needs in the digital world.[45] Readers saw capabilities like graphics and interactive as important; the print-centric organization didn't value it as much. One final example: a digital-first approach needed to pull readers into the story via a comments section. However, the *Times* had no capability for readers to do that.

More action was demanded on the processes and function of the digital-first teams. For example, many in the newsroom were under the impression that the social media team existed to promote their work while, in reality, that team was originally conceived of as primarily an information-gathering body.

All in all, the systems, processes, and people at the *Times* seemed to be inadvertently fighting the very change that might ensure their long-term survival. In terms of hearts and minds, the "head" part of the *Times* understood the need to transform, but the "heart" had trouble adapting to the change. The *New York Times* has eventually built all these capabilities and more, but other players, including the *Washington Post*, have been able to overtake them in the process.

There's one other point worth making based on the *New York Times* example of culture transformation. Building a transformative culture needs to start early in the transformation. It's too late to start building transformative culture from scratch after Stage 4 transformation because the seeds of the culture to "stay ahead" belong in the decisions made in the strategy sufficiency discipline area (chapter 8)—especially around intrapreneurship structures.

Our final example of a culture that enables perpetual transformation comes from a source who's been one of the most prolific disruptive innovators of our time—Elon Musk. In particular, the SpaceX company is a fascinating study because it illustrates the power of a common purpose.

SpaceX: How a Shared Common Purpose Can Drive an Agile Culture

SpaceX founder Elon Musk raised a lot of eyebrows in March 2018[46] when he shared that SpaceX had no business model when he started it. Neither did his next venture, the Boring Company. In fact, Musk has described starting SpaceX and Tesla, the two companies he's best known for founding, as possibly "the dumbest things to do" in terms of new ventures.[47]

The history of SpaceX, like most of Musk's ventures, is the history of vision, passion, and risk taking prevailing over conventional wisdom. SpaceX has endured many public failures. In 2006, the first SpaceX launch failed thirty-three seconds after liftoff. Its next launch in the following year failed when the rocket did not reach orbit. The year after, SpaceX's first payload for NASA ended up in the sea and almost killed the company. A 2015 launch destroyed two more NASA payloads meant for the International Space Station, and in 2016 a rocket exploded during refueling.[48] All these failures are a feature of Musk's style that prizes passion over pragmatism.

Understandably, SpaceX has had to pivot on its plans very frequently. The lack of a bigger business model may actually have been a help in those situations. How does SpaceX thrive among this orchestrated chaos?

Examining the traits of the employees that SpaceX hires provides insight into the company's highly agile culture. At the top of the four qualities they look for is an appetite for exploration. SpaceX is very clear on its mission—they exist to help mankind achieve the goal of colonizing other planets. (The other qualities are passion, drive, and talent.)

SpaceX is a fabulous example of how a common purpose can drive organizations to an agility to persevere in the face of all odds.

The Discipline of Creating an Agile Culture to Stay Ahead

The examples of Zappos, the *New York Times*, and SpaceX provide insights into what makes for a culture that provides perpetual transformation. The enterprise that facilitates the most change internally has the best chance of constantly evolving. And this constant evolution on a digital backbone of the enterprise prevents it from being a digital one-hit wonder.

It is not a coincidence that the best Silicon Valley enterprises all share these three characteristics. Procter & Gamble's NGS modeled itself after this. In part III of this book, we will see how this and other disciplines came together to deliver big wins for NGS.

Chapter Summary

- Culture eats strategy for breakfast (and apparently lunch, according to another quote). Whatever it consumes, the fact is that for an organization to digest digital transformation, there are three specific behaviors that will enable an agile culture necessary to create a living DNA of perpetual digital transformation: customer-focused innovation, an adaptive environment, and a shared common purpose.

- Building an agile culture must start early in the digital transformation process. It's too late to start after Stage 4, although it must be completed before Stage 5.

- The lessons from successful Silicon Valley companies such as Zappos have proved how culture plays a hugely disproportionate role in fostering transformation through customer-focused innovation.

- The leaked *New York Times* internal memo of 2014 on the paper's digital transformation challenges demonstrates that missing an adaptive culture can significantly slow down the natural momentum of the organization and resist digital transformation.

- The remarkable story of SpaceX and how it continues to break paradigms in its attempt to put humans on other planets is a clear case for purpose-driven agility.

Your Disciplines Checklist

Evaluate your digital transformation against the questions in figure 24 to follow a disciplined approach to each step in Digital Transformation 5.0.

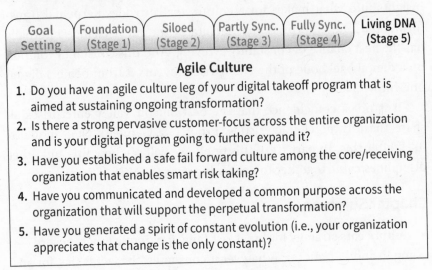

Goal Setting	Foundation (Stage 1)	Siloed (Stage 2)	Partly Sync. (Stage 3)	Fully Sync. (Stage 4)	Living DNA (Stage 5)

Agile Culture

1. Do you have an agile culture leg of your digital takeoff program that is aimed at sustaining ongoing transformation?
2. Is there a strong pervasive customer-focus across the entire organization and is your digital program going to further expand it?
3. Have you established a safe fail forward culture among the core/receiving organization that enables smart risk taking?
4. Have you communicated and developed a common purpose across the organization that will support the perpetual transformation?
5. Have you generated a spirit of constant evolution (i.e., your organization appreciates that change is the only constant)?

Figure 24 Your disciplines checklist for agile culture

Chapter 12

Sensing Risk

In the decade before I led the creation of NGS, Procter & Gamble's GBS had religiously driven constant change cycles between 2002 and 2015. The organization design was proactively tweaked every twenty-four months. Over time, the early model of saving costs via offshore services centers evolved to a mostly outsourced model. That was followed by the evolution to a fully value-driven model to provide business growth services, in addition to cost savings. The next evolution delivered additional improvements to operational excellence and speed of delivering big ideas. The NGS evolution to the fourth generation of shared services was the latest in this journey.

Though P&G's GBS had the luxury of transforming itself proactively, many of the examples cited in this book, starting with John Stephenson, did not. One of the reasons why digital transformations end up being Stage 4 "one-hit wonders" is that they don't appreciate the risk of disruption in time to transform on their own terms. Consequently, enterprises fall victim to the boiling frog syndrome (i.e., frogs jump out when placed directly in hot water but get boiled to death when placed in cool water that's boiled slowly).

The good news on the Fourth Industrial Revolution is that there are quality early-warning signals available. What's lacking is the new discipline to read them continuously.

What if there were higher-quality early-warning systems available for potential disruption? Better still, what if these were already available and the only action necessary was to be disciplined about reading them? That's the good news on the Fourth Industrial Revolution. There are quality early-warning signals available. What's lacking is the new discipline to read them continuously.

The Discipline of Measuring and Acting on Disruption Risks

The phenomenon of needing to reinvent a company isn't new. It's the accelerated frequency to reinvent that's different. Most enterprises, whether public, private, or nonprofit, already have a strategic planning process. The strategic plan is intended to capture risks, among other things. Proactive leaders sense the risk of digital disruption intuitively, like specially talented frogs in a slowly boiling vessel who think "hmmm, it's getting warm in here" (to use a really bad analogy). Adding a digital disruption metric to the strategic plan would obviate the necessity to act based on just intuition alone.

Adding a digital disruption metric to the strategic plan would obviate the necessity to act based on just intuition alone.

I call that metric the "digital disruption index." It's a composite number on a five-point scale that is the average of four individual ratings, best visualized on a spiderweb chart (see figure 25). The warning signs can come from the following risk areas:

- Your industry trends

- Your customers information

- Your business model trends

- Your digital business performance and digital organization feedback

The digital disruption index can be used to visualize these four risk elements to provide a more comprehensive measurement of threat levels. The larger the area of each of the four shapes, the higher the risk. So, in figure 25, the area for Company Performance Risk is relatively small, but the risk of two other factors—Industry and Business Model—needs attention. Reviewing the details of these risks periodically helps avoid the "boiling frog syndrome" of disruption.

P&G GBS's Intuitive Risk Identification

In 2015, when GBS president Julio Nemeth was convinced that the current model needed to be disrupted, he had based it entirely on intuition. However, when we look at GBS in light of the four risk areas

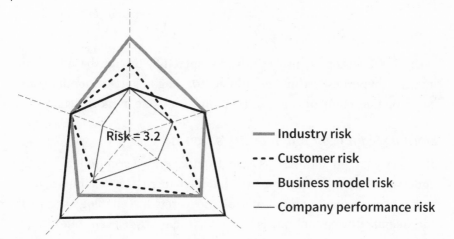

Figure 25 Digital disruption index

mentioned above, it becomes evident that there were signs that the current P&G GBS model would decline over time.

- *Industry trends*: The business process outsourcing (BPO) industry, which is a major supplier to shared services, was already showing signs of turmoil. While the global industry continued to grow, global services providers like IBM and HP were entering challenging times. Although BPO providers in India still grew, their margins had declined after the initial boom of the post-2008 recession. In parallel, the VC/start-up market was also evolving. Enterprise IT solution activity from start-up companies was growing, signaling the availability of newer generations of GBS capabilities.

- *Customer information*: The consumer electronics boom had resulted in higher expectations on user experience. In addition, the growing awareness of the urgency of digital disruption among business unit leaders meant that much more innovation was expected.

- *Business model trends*: The growing need to apply digital capabilities to the product side of the P&G business (e.g., ecommerce, digital advertising, digital supply chain, etc.) meant that business units were working directly with several IT vendors once again. The previous P&G model of the GBS/IT organization being the funnel for all digital capabilities would no longer be sufficient.

- *Business performance results*: While GBS happily continued to exceed financial and service level goals, there was a starting trend for a growing amount of the savings to be delivered by cutting project work.

Julio's decision to proactively disrupt GBS, though based on an intuitive hypothesis, can be codified for ongoing risk identification based on these four signals. Let's examine each one in more detail.

Warning Signs from Your Industry's Trends

The fact that no industry is safe from digital disruption is widely understood now. While the initial digital disruption examples may come from media, finance, entertainment, retail, technology services, and manufacturing, nobody is immune. The more relevant question is which specific processes within an industry are being disrupted, and when. There are several signals for these specific disruptions already available from industry data, including:

- Digitalization potential of core processes

- Volume of digitally native start-ups

- Number of successful disruptive start-ups

- Overall industry growth and profitability

- Adjacent industry disruption

- Venture capital business trends

Most of these indicators are easily available, but the newer source of information that I would highlight is venture capitalist data (see sidebar).

Focus on Venture Capitalist Relationships and Their Data in the Digital Era

Venture capitalists should be a transformative leader's best friend. This is a highly symbiotic relationship. VCs need feedback for their start-ups, and enterprises need the new ideas. Most VCs have personalized outreach programs for enterprises, including services such as hosting clients for "speed dating" sessions with start-ups. VCs love transformative enterprise leaders!

Most enterprise relationships with VCs fall short because they focus on their current core products or services only. That's insufficient for seeing other types of possible disruptions, i.e., disruptions in business models, as well as in operational efficiency. For instance, subscription ecommerce models in health, beauty, and personal care products have changed the very nature of the industry. Cultivating VC relationships to monitor competition only in products would have completely missed this threat.

The antidote is simple: leverage VCs for broader scanning as well as connect them deeper into your organization, where there's fuller appreciation of potential opportunities and threats. As mentioned in earlier chapters, transformative possibilities can come from product, business model, or disruptive operational capabilities. VC relationships should be holistic, covering all three areas. So for instance, if you're in the energy drink industry, then hopefully you've been monitoring for threats in nonproduct areas as well (e.g., disruptive operating trends). For example, Red Bull's social marketing prowess is affecting the energy drink industry significantly. Its success has been as much due to its enviable content marketing as its product. Whether sponsoring Felix Baumgartner's jump from the edge of space or using YouTube videos of extreme sports to connect to their three million subscribers, Red Bull's business model now relies substantially on their marketing, not just on their product.

VC data is also becoming increasingly available commercially. Sources such as Crunchbase, which has a lot of free information—from VC investment trends to details of start-ups—are a good place to start. Other sources such as CB Insights and Signals Analytics provide further customized analysis on who might be disrupting your enterprise.

Warning Signs from Your Customers

There's a common thread across many of the usual list of disruptors—Craigslist, Netflix, Hulu, Amazon, Alibaba, Uber, and others. They all identified an opportunity to improve customer experience. There's a new CX (customer experience) law of digital disruption floating around: any customer experience that involves friction points that can be improved through digitization will be.

Here's the fine print, though: the driver for change isn't necessarily how poor or expensive the previous service was; it's how much it can be improved. The newspaper classified ad experience wasn't particularly terrible. It's just that free online classifieds would always be better. That led Craigslist and other online classified ad outlets to decimate print classifieds.

The driver for change for customers isn't necessarily how poor or expensive the previous service was; it's how much it can be improved.

There's a huge difference between measuring customer satisfaction scores and customer experience. A good customer satisfaction score or a strong product performance score isn't a guarantee of undying customer loyalty. A single-minded focus on eliminating customer friction points is a better bet.

Customers have long been the most reliable sources of early-warning signals. However, beyond traditional market share information or customer satisfaction scores, there's a new breed of customer experience metrics that are more reliable indicators of potential digital disruption. Measures such as social customer influence and customer engagement, especially when monitored across adjacent industries, are a good indicator of potential disruption as well as the degree to which CX could disrupt you. The customer effort score (CES)—the amount of effort needed to accomplish a task—is another good indicator, especially when compared to digital alternatives. A high CES score says that you might be exposed to a disruption driven via CX.

So, the metrics that should be included in the customer experience digital risk index are:

- Customer experience digitalization potential

- Customer service friction points

- Social customer influence, customer engagement

- Customer effort score

Warning Signs from Your Business Model

Leaders already know which business model threats could upend their organizations. The stories of companies being "Uber-ed" overnight might make for good reading but, in reality, don't hold up to close scrutiny. The issue for most organizations isn't the awareness of the threat to their current business model; it is the underestimation of the proximity of the threat.

The fact is that any attempt by nimble competition to better meet your customers' needs—usually via an alternative path to market or method of value creation—can eventually disrupt your business model. The only question is timing.

Measuring the trends in alternative business models via the following provides a good indication on how imminent the business model changes are:

- Channel evolution

- Value proposition changes

- Shifts among start-ups on key activities for business execution

- Shifts in key resources used for the business

- Changes in possible partnerships

Warning Signs from Digital Business Performance and Digital Organization Feedback

These metrics reflect the levels of digital investment and its results in your products, processes, and people. A seminal study in 2015 by the IBM Institute for Business Value called "Redefining Boundaries—Insights from the Global C-suite Study"[49] collected and analyzed data from more than 28,000 interviews with C-suite executives. They identified the "Torchbearers," approximately 5 percent of their respondents with strong innovation reputations who outperformed their peers in terms of revenue growth and profitability. Based on their analysis, Torchbearers invested 24 to 40 percent more than Market Followers on "big-bet" emerging technologies. Torchbearers also paid 22 percent more attention to feedback from their customers than Market Followers, mostly by paying 22 percent less attention to direct competitors.

In addition to measuring the levels of investments in emerging technology, you also need to examine where your major technology investments are going. If most of the tech investment (in both IT and non-IT budgets) has been directed toward improving the bottom line, that may be a problem. Enterprises don't necessarily need the exact Google ratio of 70-20-10 between operational costs, continuous improvement costs, and disruptive innovation costs. But if the enterprise is unable to reinvest a significant chunk of productivity savings into customer service, growing the business, and creating new business models, then it is at risk of a downward spiral toward digital disruption.

The digital investment metrics here should include the following:

- Levels of investment in emerging technology

- Investments in a digital workforce

- Percentage of the business that is digitally based

- Amount of digital investment that is ultimately customer focused

- How much of the digital investments are sustainable ongoing

On the last point about sustainable digital investments, there may be a need to "save to reinvest," i.e., drive further savings (including in other IT areas) to free up the cash.

Why Are the Warning Signals Ignored?

As mentioned earlier, leaders have a sense of their organization's digital disruption peril already. The bigger question is how much they are reacting to it, and if not enough, then why. The answer to this tends to be sociological—fear, inertia, and misjudgment. Fear about cannibalizing existing products and about the cost of change. Inertia caused by complacency that the current strategy has historically worked. And finally, misjudgment on the potential impact of digital disruption and an optimistic view of the organization's ability to withstand the new competition. In the rest of the chapter, I dig deeper into these factors and suggest an antidote—a disciplined approach to address this as part of the annual strategic planning processes.

Fear

Concerns about product cannibalization, the high cost of change, and risk to operations tend to be endemic to the prevailing culture and, to be fair, may arise from the nature of the industry and its business model (especially in industries that get high scrutiny, e.g., defense, finance, health care, etc.). The answer isn't to become reckless risk takers but to have a disciplined approach to balancing governance expectations with disruptive innovation. Disruptive start-ups haven't shied away from these industries, which implies that disciplined disruption is possible. The real risk is to let these concerns become a hindrance for change, as is illustrated by the case studies on Bausch & Lomb and Research In Motion in the sidebar.

How Fear of Change Can Cost You

A healthy respect for the complexity of change is good, but fear of change is not. Here are a couple examples of situations where avoiding change backfired.

- *Fear of cannibalizing existing products:* Leonardo da Vinci is reputed to have first suggested the idea of contact lenses in his 1508 *Codex of the eye, Manual D*. It wasn't until the late 1800s that scientists were able to come up with glass and eventually plastic contact lenses. However, the major issue with these hard contacts was that they did not allow oxygen to penetrate to the cornea and conjunctiva, causing serious eye problems. That's why the invention of soft contacts was such a breakthrough. Bausch & Lomb acquired the licenses to manufacture soft contacts around 1965 and ran into a dilemma. If they pushed soft contacts too hard, they risked cannibalizing their lucrative drops for hard lenses. It wasn't until Johnson & Johnson stepped into this gap that the inevitability of soft contacts was realized. Hard lenses and their drops were doomed, and Bausch & Lomb had to scramble to catch up.

- *Fear of the cost of change:* In the early 2000s, Research In Motion (RIM) ruled the world in smart multifeature phone devices. RIM offered unprecedented, reliable capabilities to its customers, combining outstanding performance and security based on its proprietary operating system (OS) and hardware. Then the iPhone came along in 2007. RIM and all its existing competitors—Nokia, Microsoft, and Palm—were faced with tough choices on both OS design and touchscreen capabilities. Unlike RIM, most of these competitors weren't as entrenched in their OS investments and could pivot. RIM was also faced with a strategic dilemma on whether to rely on their historical strengths of security and a beloved keyboard interface or go with the flow of the newer user experience. RIM had a much bigger cost of changing its OS and was slow to move in the direction that their users were dictating. As a result, RIM's sales peaked in 2010 and then declined dramatically after that.

Inertia

Unlike the sociological factor of a fear of change which is driven by a desire to be cautious about the effects of modification, inertia has no redeeming qualities, especially in the digital era. The root causes of complacency and an endemic lack of urgency will eventually have significant consequences. Clayton Christensen's groundbreaking work, *The Innovator's Dilemma* (see sidebar), helps explain some of the factors behind inertia not just in individual organizations but also in entire industries. However, the intent here is to explain, not justify, inertia and to raise awareness of its threat in the digital era.

Inertia in Changing Old Business Models in the Energy Sector

Clayton Christensen's 1997 book *The Innovator's Dilemma* went a long way toward helping leaders understand how strategies that made organizations extremely successful could harbor the seeds of eventual disruption. The Fourth Industrial Revolution has made that dynamic even more urgent. Sectors facing disruption in the short and medium term, like energy, are seeing different players react very differently to disrupting their own business models. Some of the better-run companies are placing big bets on alternative energy.

That's good to see, because for decades the big energy companies invested heavily in political and consumer influence—including denying the proven science of climate change—to prop up their oil-based business model. That's changing dramatically. Onshore wind energy generation is already the cheapest source of energy in many places. In India, solar energy at a cost of sixty-five cents per watt (roughly half the cost in the US) is already cheaper than coal. As with other disruptive technologies, such as cell phones, the developing markets are taking the opportunity to leapfrog technology. Additionally, in sub-Saharan Africa, companies such as M-KOPA in Kenya are creating entirely new business models. These build on the ability to eliminate reliance on expensive energy grids by generating solar energy on site.

The ability to get moving against old business models and practices will determine which companies become the energy giants of the future.

Misjudgment

Even very smart people will occasionally make huge mistakes when grappling with the future. Consider the confident prediction in 2007 of Steve Ballmer, CEO of Microsoft: "There's no chance that the iPhone is going to get any significant market share." He wasn't the only smart person to misjudge a trend. The sidebar has several other entertaining examples.

The issue of misjudgment is often related to the fact that the human mind finds it easier to comprehend linear increments (e.g., 1, 2, 3, 4, 5 . . .) rather than exponential increments (1, 2, 4, 8, 16, 32 . . .). The classic example here is Kodak, which invented the first digital camera in 1975 but chose not to push digital photography at the time.[50] Instead, in 1981 Sony introduced the first electronic camera. Kodak's market research at the time estimated that they had at least ten years before the digital impact would become significant. Although that was correct, what was missed was the exponential growth of digital technology after impact. The exponential pace after a decade meant that catching up became close to impossible. It's critical to watch for exponential trends.

Smart People Who Got Predictions Wrong . . .

"Television won't be able to hold on to any market it captures after the first six months. People will soon get tired of staring at a plywood box every night."

—Darryl Zanuck, executive at 20th Century Fox, 1946

"The horse is here to stay but the automobile is only a novelty—a fad."

> —President of the Michigan Savings Bank advising Henry Ford's lawyer, Horace Rackham, not to invest in the Ford Motor Company, 1903

> *"The Americans have need of the telephone, but we do not. We have plenty of messenger boys."*
> —Sir William Preece, Chief Engineer, British Post Office, 1876

> *"I think there is a world market for maybe five computers."*
> —Thomas Watson, president of IBM, 1943

> *"There is no reason anyone would want a computer in their home."*
> —Ken Olsen, founder of Digital Equipment Corporation, 1977

> These were all brilliant people who misjudged either the timing of the disruption or the strength of their countermeasures.

The Discipline of Addressing Fear, Inertia, and Misjudgment

Enterprises that plan to sustain their superiority after digital transformation can address these risks systemically with a slight tweak to their annual strategy planning exercise. I introduced the metric of the digital disruption index earlier in the chapter. This must be incorporated into the annual strategy planning. Specifically, the competitive intelligence assessment within the strategy exercise should include a thorough review of the digital disruption index as well as plans to address threats adequately.

Reviewing the absolute score of the digital disruption index and its trend provides discipline on how urgently to react.

Chapter Summary

- Separating the hype on digital disruption from reality is a challenge. When, where, and how much to react to disruptive threats is a dilemma. Act ineffectively and you risk wasting your resources and being disrupted anyway.

- The digital disruption index provides a disciplined metric to sense and address the risk of digital disruption on an ongoing basis. It includes measurement across four areas:

▶ *Industry trends:* Beyond the usual metrics, look for trends in VC investments as well. Also, invest in the data sources that are used by VCs to help you focus on the right disruptions.

▶ *Customers*: Customers of your enterprise and those in adjoining industries will provide the best data. Newer metrics, such as customer experience and customer effort score, indicate possibilities for disruptions in the business model.

▶ *Business model:* Assessing parts of the current business model, such as evolution of channels, partners, and activity systems, can provide useful insights on threats.

▶ *Digital business and organization:* Understanding the state of investments in digital business and digital literacy helps give a sense of the risk of underreaction to digital disruption.

▪ Sociological issues such as fear, inertia, and misjudgment explain why action against digital risks is often insufficient. The discipline of adding the digital disruption index metric to the annual strategy planning exercise can help.

Your Disciplines Checklist

Evaluate your digital transformation against the questions in figure 26 to follow a disciplined approach to each step in Digital Transformation 5.0.

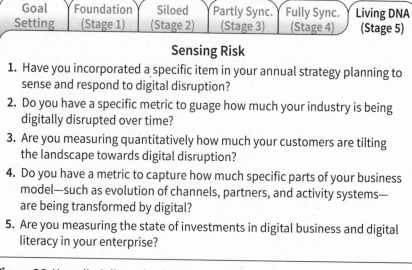

Goal Setting	Foundation (Stage 1)	Siloed (Stage 2)	Partly Sync. (Stage 3)	Fully Sync. (Stage 4)	Living DNA (Stage 5)

Sensing Risk

1. Have you incorporated a specific item in your annual strategy planning to sense and respond to digital disruption?

2. Do you have a specific metric to guage how much your industry is being digitally disrupted over time?

3. Are you measuring quantitatively how much your customers are tilting the landscape towards digital disruption?

4. Do you have a metric to capture how much specific parts of your business model—such as evolution of channels, partners, and activity systems—are being transformed by digital?

5. Are you measuring the state of investments in digital business and digital literacy in your enterprise?

Figure 26 Your disciplines checklist for sensing risk

Part III

Winning with Digital Transformation

Chapter 13

P&G's NGS Transformation

The final two chapters in the book build upon my conviction that when it comes to thriving in the Fourth Industrial Revolution, fortune favors the disciplined and prepared mind. The digital revolution is literally the opportunity of a lifetime. It's up to us to seize it and to be disciplined enough to succeed. To illustrate how all the surprising disciplines to take off and stay ahead can come together, I show how the various jigsaw pieces of the disciplines were assembled at P&G's Next Generation Services.

P&G's Quest for Transformation of Its Global Business Services

The Human Genome Project cost $2.5 billion in 2003 to sequence the first genome. Prices have fallen exponentially to the extent that I get junk mail in my in-box quoting $100 to sequence my genome. When was the last time the cost of IT services dropped way beyond 99 percent in fifteen years? And why shouldn't the global business services industry, which is essentially a data business, not be experiencing exponential capability increases?

This was the question on my mind when I started working on NGS in 2015. P&G's GBS had industry best-in-class benchmarks, but there had to be a way for us to find the next S-curve of improvement. To stimulate ideas, we talked with more than a hundred organizations—peer shared services organizations, consultancies, IT providers, VCs, and start-ups. One of those happened to be an Australian-based global software company with revenues of $500 million. I asked them if they had a shared services organization. They did not. I knew they were incredibly efficient in their operations, so I persisted in questioning them on how they ran their HR services like payroll, hiring, and performance management. They said that their HR function operated these. My next question was how large their HR organization was across their ten physical country locations. Their answer blew me away—twenty-five people. More incredibly, they read the surprise on my face and thought that number was too high! They said somewhat defensively that half their HR was dedicated to hiring, since the company was doubling their head count each year. While I picked up my jaw from where it had fallen to the floor, I realized that I had stumbled upon an important insight— the next generation of shared services already existed. It was how digitally native companies ran their internal operations.

A Digital Backbone of Operations

The next few months would throw up example after example of why a digital backbone to the company's operation in the future was not just desirable but was already starting to exist in the new generation of digitally savvy companies. Benchmark costs of IT and shared services as a percentage of revenue in those companies were less than half of those in large companies. A major wealth and asset management company in New York had doubled its employee productivity four times in the previous ten years. The examples mentioned earlier in the book— including x.ai, the robot admin who was able to do calendaring, or bots writing 90 percent of the short online updates on stock prices or sports results, or ShotSpotter, the AI tool used to triangulate the location of gunshots fired in real time using camera information, and many more—suddenly emerged in support of the concept of a digital backbone of operations.

Digital transformation in most organizations will take three forms—new digital business models (e.g., from retail to online selling), new technology-embedded products (e.g., driverless cars), and digital internal operations (e.g., using AI for wealth management). The future of GBS, including the IT function, was to transform itself to be the digital core of operations in the entire enterprise.

Our research uncovered dozens of disruptive possibilities within the shared services industry to support the goal of GBS becoming the digital core of P&G's operations. The example of travel expense solutions in digitally native organizations, including Google, Adobe, Netflix, among others, was eye-opening. Most traditional enterprises have rigorous standards on where to book flights and which hotels to stay in. After each trip, all expenses are meticulously documented in expense reports—a chore that most travelers hate.

The process followed by some digitally native organizations was radically different. Before each trip, the traveler logged onto a system and entered the destination and the dates of the trip. Based on a huge database of anticipated costs, the system then provided a trip budget. The traveler was free to book their tickets at any site and allowed to stay anywhere. Their corporate credit card had details of expenses already, and therefore the system didn't need the employee to create an expense report. Further, if the trip budget was underspent, the policy allowed the traveler to put the savings to use in flexible ways—including staying at a posh hotel during the next trip or even donating the savings to charity. These practices not only saved the enterprise money (up to 30 percent) and eliminated noncore activities in the enterprise (e.g., managing travel agencies, negotiating hotel deals, matching expense receipts to claims) but also improved employee satisfaction for having given them an adult business deal.

Over the next three years of my leadership of NGS, we would run about twenty-five projects of similar 10X potential. We would run these as a portfolio mix where some projects were killed if they did not meet speed and financial criteria and others that overachieved their initial potential. As long as the portfolio as a whole over-delivered its goals, we were fine. The possibilities in creating a digital core of enterprise operations were endless. Here are a few examples:

- Can you run the supply chain planning operations of an enterprise, end to end from supply to demand, and in real time? The standard practices in the world today treat every process in manufacturing resource planning (MRP) as siloed exercises involving demand forecasting, demand planning, manufacturing execution planning, transportation planning, and so on. The siloed optimization of these processes in large global manufacturing enterprises can result in thousands of employees filling in the gaps. That's archaic in today's world, where modern technology architectures can handle trillions of events per hour and use thousands of AI algorithms to optimize plans across the whole system in real time.

- How about a "Siri"-like experience for all enterprise systems, with the ability to cut across siloed systems in the enterprise to provide the solution to most needs? So for instance, instead of going to several individual systems when planning for a new hire to join the company (e.g., security badge, salary, facilities, PC and email, training systems, etc.), could we simply say "Hey Siri, set up a new hire, Jane Smith, to start on March 1, 2020" and then have the process executed across all siloed systems after providing a few more details. This same user experience would be available for business transactions as well.

- Could AI be used to dramatically redesign accounts receivables processes? Instead of hundreds of employees in large organizations manually executing processes such as deciding which of the disputes for underpayment from customer companies were valid, could we have algorithms make those decisions?

- Could algorithms ingest incoming contract documents from suppliers and red-line (highlight) parts of the proposal that were not compliant with policy or were areas for negotiation?

- Could financial forecasts be done more accurately by algorithms than by a combination of the traditional forecasting systems and humans?

- Could an AI brain for the purchasing function guide buyers in chosen spend pools on their most complex decisions? For instance, keeping up with supplier and industry changes, identifying pricing trends in real time, and even placing spot-buying orders? Or driving more competition among suppliers by ingesting more external data on new supplier possibilities? And in matching ongoing invoices and payments against complicated pricing tables in contracts to avoid overpayment?

- Could we disrupt the entire call center experience using algorithms that could translate from voice to text and search vast internal knowledge bases for answers to complex issues, and in the process provide more service and more choices to users?

- Could we eliminate 90 percent or more of all IT outages in the enterprise (i.e., from power supply to network, server, database, data quality, or user experience outages) by gathering signals related to the operation of these in a massive data lake and then using algorithms to predict and self-heal most of the issues? And could we do this simultaneously across the world and across all suppliers?

- Could complex global ocean shipping and air transportation across countries and suppliers be made more transparent and simple, especially on the current status of location of goods and actual cost of transportation, and possibly even eliminate the need for suppliers to send invoices?

- Could video technology be used to do actual "observed" consumer behavior instead of "claimed" behavior by using video algorithms to trawl through massive volumes of footage and provide data based on actual actions of customers? Observing actual behavior is more reliable than asking people how they might behave in a situation. Doing this at massive scale today is a huge challenge.

- Could the massive challenge of synchronizing "master data" in the enterprise (e.g., standard codes and values such as the correct weight or the right SKU code for a product anywhere in the world) be finally fixed?

Hundreds of opportunities along these lines exist in the enterprise and are viable ideas. Whether a given organization can execute any, some, or all of them is a different question. It's the difference between identifying a viable end state and executing digital transformation successfully. The big question is how to transition from a stable, successful current state to a highly desirable but uncertain future state.

The Challenge of Transition

The question of successfully transitioning from current to future state brings us back full circle to the question of why digital transformations fail. The lessons from the NGS journey have led to the creation of the five-stage model of digital transformation. In particular, I would like to highlight the example of three disciplines that played a critical role at the start of the NGS program.

Strategy Sufficiency

The NGS goals were ambitious—we would disrupt P&G's GBS, but in the process change the entire shared services industry. That raised the issue of strategy sufficiency. How could a small group of P&G folks disrupt an entire industry? The best strategy in our case was to create an ecosystem effect.

First, NGS had to be more than just a P&G-only group. No matter how strong our group of internal resources, a broader ecosystem of resources would always deliver more transformative capabilities than any one company could. We agreed to define NGS as an open ecosystem that would have three groups:

- A dozen or so P&G handpicked resources who would design the 10X ideas and implement them in the base organization.

- A half-dozen or so current P&G IT partners like EY, Genpact, Infosys, L&T Infotech, HCL, HPE/DXC, Tata Consultancy Services, and WNS. They would scale up the 10X ideas into products.

- A large ecosystem of start-ups brought to NGS via ten of the top VCs in the world. They would bring in the latest disruptive capabilities, which could be complemented and "enterprise hardened" by the IT partners and implemented by the P&G NGS leaders.

Second, the ecosystem would have to be based on a win-win relationship for all participants. The value proposition with the P&G IT partners was as follows—they would bring in the resources and the product development funding needed to create the 10X software product. In return, they would get the intellectual property and the rights to sell the products externally to other companies (that didn't compete directly with P&G). If the product was truly a 10X digital transformative to P&G's GBS—a best-in-class shared services organization—then it had to be very commercially appealing to others. The value proposition for the start-ups was to get a foothold at an attractive client in return for co-innovating with us. And the win for P&G was to get 10X disruptions at low to no cost.

Third, even this ecosystem of the three groups would not be large enough to disrupt at large scale. We would therefore need a bigger community and a crowd to support it. Most of the ideas as well as execution capacity for NGS would come from these. The "community" included passionate people within P&G and its immediate partners who were attracted by the high quality of the work and wanted to be a part of it. The "crowd" included unlimited resources available from crowdsourcing the work—via universities, start-up communities, and specialist groups like Kaggle for analytics problems.

Iterative Execution

The NGS operating model was defined very early on to be an iterative, high-risk, high-return execution.

First, NGS would focus only on 10X disruptive initiatives. The core organization would take on day-to-day continuous improvement work.

Second, inspired by Alphabet/Google X, the NGS operation was set up to be a portfolio of projects. As owner of the organization, I saw my role to be like a venture capitalist for the projects. For every ten experiments (projects) I took on, I would kill five, expect to have another four deliver only 2X outcomes, and have one turn out to be a 10X disruption.

Third, to create a rapid "clock speed" of operation, we agreed to a general guideline for duration of each stage of work. This was based on the exponential series of 1-2-4-8-16: one month for landscape assessment, two months for design, four months for hypothesis testing, eight months to complete development and all in-market testing, and sixteen months to complete all deployments.

Finally, the operating model itself for the ideation and deployment were standardized to use design thinking and lean startup.

Change Management Model

The chosen model was to create an "edge" organization that would be made up of handpicked, highly credible operational leaders chartered to drive change in the core organization but would operate behind a "cultural firewall" on the initial stages of each project to reward high-risk, high-return experiments.

The choice of who to assign to NGS was made with change management in mind. The dozen leaders were handpicked by the GBS leadership, based primarily on their high credibility within the core organization as opposed to their technical skills or innovative abilities. These leaders worked full-time with NGS but focused on experiments that were high value (usually a $50 million potential or more) and were critical innovation priorities within their individual organizations' annual strategic plan. To enable the focus on speed (vs. policy compliance) during early stages of each project, the team was allowed to operate behind a "cultural firewall" that promoted smart risk taking at earlier stages of the projects while protecting them from the natural corporate immune system.

By the end of my role after three years in NGS, the actual results followed the 10-5-4-1 model extremely well. Of the twenty-five odd experiments (projects) that were undertaken, four were definitely 10X and eight were 2X to 5X in nature. For every instance of success, there were two or more that failed. That's where the culture of rewarding "learn by doing" kicked in. There was no failure—only learning, as long as the portfolio effect of all these experiments (projects) continued to exceed overall financial goals. The decision to place the transformation-leading organization at the headquarters in Cincinnati instead of in Silicon Valley was a brilliant move. At the end of the day, digital transformation is less about the technical capabilities and more about systemically changing people's thinking. That may have been among the biggest side effects of having established NGS—the inspiration to the rest of the organization that transformation was not just desirable, but that each person could actually contribute to it and lead it within their own roles.

Chapter Summary

- Any motivated organization can approach digital transformation using the example of P&G's Next Generation Services.

- Digital transformation can take three forms: entirely new business models (e.g., from physical retail to online), technology-driven new products (e.g., driverless cars), and digital operations. The specific case study from NGS was about creating new digital operations.

- The challenge for most leaders is how to transition from current state to a desired future state. That's where the five-stage model for digital transformation can help.

Chapter 14

How Digital Transformations Can Succeed

I'm a huge optimist when it comes to the digital era. I believe that the new digital tools have the potential to transform people, enterprises, and society. I'm also a realist when it comes to the disruptive power of digital. Like all the disruptive tools of the previous industrial revolutions, it will generate the pain of change. The question is not whether digital disruption will occur but what role we want to play when it does.

My intent is to share how diligence is the mother of good fortune, to quote Miguel de Cervantes, especially when applied to digital transformation.

Why Digital Transformations Fail *provides a blueprint for successful transformation. It puts the digital transformation journey into context and provides a disciplined road map to move up the stages of transformation via the five-stage digital transformation model.*

Targeting the right ideal stage (i.e., Stage 5) is only the start of the journey. It's equally important to follow a disciplined approach to get there. That's the role of the surprising disciplines. I call these disciplines surprising because one would assume that the key to success on digital transformation is creativity in coming up with new business models and in transforming the organization. My own experience has taught me that this is insufficient. The real key to success in digital transformation is discipline. The aspiration of Why Digital Transformations Fail *is to bring rigor in execution to help make digital transformations successful.*

Thriving in the Fourth Industrial Revolution is absolutely possible. There's a myth that Abraham Lincoln, Steve Jobs, and Peter Drucker have something in common because they are all quoted for having said some variation of "the best way to predict the future is to create it." Regardless of claims of their originality, they were all correct. As digital continues to drive an unprecedented pace of change, the modern equivalent is probably "the best way to prevent being Uber-ed is to be the Uber-er."

To be clear, our motivations for leading change don't need to be defensive. To the contrary, every change is an opportunity, and the world has never seen as much opportunity as that driven by the Fourth Industrial Revolution.

Digital Is an Opportunity of Historic Proportions

When Marc Andreessen published his article in the *Wall Street Journal* in August 2011 titled "Why Software Is Eating the World," most traditional leaders found it hard to equate what was happening at Amazon, Pixar, Apple, or Netflix with the future of their own companies. That was understandable. As Bill Gates said famously, "We always overestimate the change that will occur in the next two years and underestimate the change that will occur in the next ten." It hasn't been ten years yet from the publication of Andreessen's article, but his meaning is now suddenly clear. Digital disruption isn't just for the tech or media or entertainment industries alone. It is so widely accepted that software will disrupt every industry that newspaper articles now list which industries have been *least* disrupted. And even those are scraping the bottom of the barrel when they list government and judiciary as being relatively untouched by digital disruption.

All that industrial transformation is an opportunity of historic proportions. Software is eating the world, not in a destructive Pac-Man way, but more in the manner of plants that consume carbon dioxide and light to generate oxygen. We see signs of this digital photosynthesis all around us. Digital is multiplying the capabilities of all other disruptors, whether nanotech or drones or solar. Examples of these abound. The sheer breadth of what's possible today and how quickly it changes is breathtaking. I share a tiny percentage of such examples below.

- Five of the top ten companies in the world by market capitalization in 2018, per PwC, are technology companies. And that doesn't include Amazon or Alibaba, which are classified as "consumer services."

- Eight years ago only one of these ten, Microsoft, was on the top ten list.

- Autonomous vehicles, which seemed like science fiction only a few years ago, will account for about $50 billion in sales by 2035. The children being born today may never need to apply for a driver's license.

- Warehousing, which used to be a heavily manual operation, is now significantly automated. Gone are the days when a human picker went to the toothbrush, deodorant, and lipstick aisle to fulfill your online order for these three products. Today, instead of the picker moving to the aisles, robots move the shelves to the stationary picker.

- Additive manufacturing, like 3D printing, will account for 10 percent of all manufacturing in the next ten years. China has already 3D printed a six-story building. The International Space Station has been printing tools and spare parts for itself for years now.

- Software algorithm-based supply chain planning will dramatically shrink the product inventories and lead times in supply chains. The fashion retailer Zara has been delivering fashion from designer ideas to retail stock within two weeks for several years now.

- Agile, custom-built manufacturing will slowly replace large-scale "batch" manufacturing. Chinese smartphone manufacturer Xiaomi already ships new batches of phones every week, with each batch having superior capabilities to the last. They also register 70 percent of their sales online, including preorders, which allows them to purchase raw material only after sales have been placed.

- Nearly 40 percent of all jobs in the financial services sector could be done by software robots by 2030.

- Between 40 to 50 percent of jobs in the manufacturing, transportation, and retail sectors could be done by hardware or software robots by 2030.

- Even robots in manufacturing will be disrupted in the next ten years as 3D printing takes over. If you can print your PC or smartphone at home, you eliminate robots in the factory.

- Average pretax income in these sectors will rise due to these productivity gains, although perhaps not equally spread between all groups of workers.

- Wealth management advice fueled by artificial intelligence (AI) will explode over the next few years. By 2025, 10 percent of all wealth being managed will use a combination of AI and humans. Of that, 16 percent of that will be managed only by robots.

- Certain news agencies already generate 90 percent of their short, pro-forma real-time news updates on sports and financial markets using software robots. AI, with some human journalist help, will generate 90 percent of all news in fifteen years.

- Voice recognition is already three times faster and more accurate than typing. In the future, natural language processing (NLP) bots will understand and execute most of the day-to-day tasks at home and at work.

- Ambient computing will explode. It is the trend of pervasively embedding computers into everyday devices to the extent that we stop thinking of computers as individual boxes.

- Deep learning, a cutting-edge subset of AI that is used in self-driving cars, will also be used to self-generate cryptographic algorithms to communicate between devices that are extremely difficult to hack.

- Deep learning can already read your lips with more than 90 percent accuracy, whereas the average lip reader usually delivers 50 percent accuracy.

- If deep learning can figure out how to play computer games without being taught or programmed, then AI-driven product development for R&D departments is already within reach.

- The gig economy—the trend of part-time or temporary employ-ment "gigs"—accounted for about 10 percent of the US workforce in 2005. It is already a third of the workforce today and expected to exceed 40 percent by 2020. You can win big by leveraging this trend.

- Thirty-two million people in the US cannot read a road sign, but by 2020 we project to have ten million self-driving cars that will accu-rately read all signs.

- By 2027, machine literacy—the ability for computers to be above basic human literacy levels—will exceed that of twenty-four million US citizens.

- Ninety percent of the global population above the age of six will have a cell phone by 2020.

- By 2030, 1.2 billion Indians will have smartphones (not just cell phones). And this is in a country where even landlines were a rarity just thirty years ago.

- Studies have consistently proven that digital technologies are narrowing the education gap in developing nations. Add that to the 90 percent global cell phone ownership levels among people six years old and up in 2020 and you have a dramatically different consumer profile to market to by 2020.

- In twenty to thirty years, the cost of producing energy at home will be a fraction of the cost of buying it off the grid.

- More importantly, it's the consequences of cheap electricity that are more exciting. Cheap electricity means cheap drinking water, as energy allows you to process all kinds of water, including seawater.

- Dozens of new battery technologies ranging from bioenergy to graphene and micro-supercapacitors will pump new life into traditional lithium-ion battery technology. Medium term, technologies like lithium-air, lithium-sulfur, and vanadium flow will likely get us to a fully renewable future in twenty years.

- Improvements in health care mean that the average American male lifespan in 2050 could be eighty-three to eighty-five years. For women, it would be eighty-nine to ninety-four years.

- By 2020, we may see human trials of surgical nanobots. These tiny robots can capture individual cells, coordinate with each other, deliver targeted medicine, and purge themselves when the job is complete.

- Medical diagnostics will become a self-serve industry, as smartphone extensions will allow patients to diagnose everything from A-fib (atrial fibrillation of the heart) to genetic disorders right at home.

- In the next five years, there will be apps that can tell by your facial expression if you're lying. Imagine what that could do to the judicial system!

- Smart cities will use sensors and digital capabilities to manage traffic, utilities, law enforcement, medical support, and other community services. There are already more than 250 smart city projects in the world today.

- India has a plan to build one hundred smart cities.

- Lab-grown cultured meat will deliver superior alternatives to conventional meat, using 50 percent less energy and 80 to 90 percent fewer emissions. That's good because the meat industry accounts for 18 percent of all our greenhouse gas emissions.

- Robots and drones are likely to be the farm workers of the future, including on small- and medium-size farms. Robots can be made for $500 in developing markets already, and this price tag will quickly fall below the $100 level.

- Virtual bartenders are already in use. Royal Caribbean's cruise ship *Anthem of the Seas* mixes your cocktails and allows you to go beyond the menu to create your own cocktails.

- Blockchain, currently the only technology claimed to be incorruptible, may finally give us secure online voting.

- Blockchain will disrupt the need for middlemen to complete financial transactions. According to the World Economic Forum, 10 percent of global GDP will be conducted over blockchain by 2025.

- A combination of full trust capability, transparency, and security will turn the manufacturing supply chains of the future into demand chains.

- In developing markets, the use of low-cost blockchains will help address endemic institutional weaknesses. Examples include expanding the sharing economy to enhance local bargaining power, growing microfinancing, attacking middleman-based corruption, and delivering secure identity and ownership documents.

- Over the next decade, modern manufacturing in the US will create 3.5 million new jobs. The big challenge will be to retrain existing workers more than threats from globalization. Up to two million high-tech manufacturing jobs may go unfilled.

- Spending on digital advertising in the US has already overtaken TV advertising in 2017. Corporate advertising functions will evolve to become data- and algorithm-driven personalized customer engagement functions.

- The corporate HR function will need a makeover to evolve away from delivering policies, processes, and talent management services. Those will be automated using HR tech. HR will evolve into delivering innovative, agile, digitally savvy human capital.

The Race to Turn Opportunity into Success

The question for forward-thinking leaders is how to turn these unprecedented opportunities into relevant action. Although the William Gibson saying "the future is already here—it's just not very evenly distributed" has always been true, the sheer discontinuity of the emerging future allows change leaders to win disproportionately versus change resistors. That's true of individuals and it's also true of organizations.

To be sure, one of the reasons why digital transformations fail is that it is hard to drive change within established enterprises. Beyond all the issues of managing change in a legacy organization and culture, the financial risk-reward systems in larger enterprises appear to be stacked against them in favor of their nimble start-up competitors. As Maxwell Wessel points out in his September 2017 article in *Harvard Business Review* titled "Why Preventing Disruption in 2017 Is Harder Than It Was When Christensen Coined the Term,"[51] the most disruptive challenges for established companies today come from start-ups that are able to create asset-light disruptions. Consider Uber vs. General Motors, or AirBnb vs. Hilton. Further, whereas larger enterprises are usually constrained to funding innovation using debt, their start-up peers borrow at 10X to 30X revenue multiples using equity stakes. Much of this cheap, asset-light disruption is enabled by digital technology. However, this dynamic cuts both ways.

Digital Is the Ultimate Leveler of the Playing Field

There are ways to even the odds within established enterprises. They do have financial wherewithal and industry knowledge and huge supportive ecosystems and select talent. Better yet, this democratization of change driven by asset-light digital models can be an equal enabler in established organizations, if applied correctly. The good news about the digital era is that it enables huge ecosystems for innovation. That can level the playing field.

One way to win disproportionately in the digital era is to be among the digital change leaders. Make your digital transformation initiative count. This book demonstrates how to improve the odds of digital transformation by lowering the costs and risk of change.

The Rest Is Up to You

We are fortunate to have the opportunity to lead change in only the fourth industrial revolution in the history of mankind. The technology is here. The change models exist. The conviction and mindset to thrive in this era will belong to individual leaders, as has always been the case throughout history. As you take up the challenge to transform the future, my humble wish would be that we learn from past stories. Digital disruption can be overcome. The reason why digital transformations fail is that they take more discipline than one might expect. It takes a surprising amount of discipline and a positive outlook of the possibilities for digital transformations to succeed.

Resource A

Checklist of the Surprising Disciplines

Table A-1 provides a template of the surprising disciplines to take off and stay ahead on digital transformation.

Table A-1 Checklist of the surprising disciplines

Stage	Discipline	Questions
	Goal Setting	1. Does the proposed transformation use two or more of the following: exponential technologies, outcome-based models, or exponential ecosystems?
		2. Is the goal of your transformation to reinvent, as opposed to create incremental evolution?
		3. Is the goal to deliver one or more of the following: new business model transformation, new technology-enabled product adjacency, or 10X operating efficiencies?
		4. Is the intent of the transformation to drive a perpetual culture of transformation?
		5. Is the proposed transformation enterprise-wide, based on a formal strategy, and driven from the top?
Foundation (Stage 1)	Committed Ownership	1. Is there complete and visible personal ownership of the digital strategy from the leader?
		2. Are there signs or plans in place for the leader to personally demonstrate new transformational behaviors?
		3. Are there structures in place to ensure that the leader translates business goals into transformation strategies and to personally engage in these going forward?

Table A-1 Checklist of the surprising disciplines (*continued*)

Stage	Discipline	Questions
Foundation (Stage 1) *Continued*	Committed Ownership	4. Is there a mechanism in place for stakeholders to transparently understand issues during transformation and to break barriers constantly?
		5. Do your sponsors and senior leaders have sufficient digital literacy to drive the transformation?
	Iterative Execution	1. Are you using an iterative, agile methodology like lean startup for execution of the project?
		2. Have you grouped your program into a portfolio of projects in a manner that allows for an optimal mix of high-risk and low-risk efforts?
		3. Has your digital transformation set up "innovation velocity" as a goal, and are there metrics associated with speed?
		4. Are there mechanisms such as the NGS 1-2-4-8-16 to help you drive speed/ innovation velocity on your projects?
		5. Is there some method to address the "two-worlds" issue to allow the transformation to progress with lower overhead and faster speed than the core organization?
Siloed (Stage 2)	Disruption Empowerment	1. Has a clear massive transformative purpose (MTP) been defined?
		2. Have the change leaders been informed about which specific elements of air cover they will receive as they drive change?
		3. Have the ancillary stakeholders and the change-affected been informed of their role to help the change?
		4. Has the leader identified and committed to personal skin in the game for the transformation?

Table A-1 Checklist of the surprising disciplines (*continued*)

Stage	Discipline	Questions
Siloed (Stage 2) *Continued*	**Disruption Empowerment**	5. Has the leader "primed the pump" for change with a few initiatives to drive the momentum?
	Digital Leverage Points	1. Have you examined all potential digital leverage areas, including creating new business models, new products, and disruptive operational excellence?
		2. Have you considered leverage possibilities external to your organization, including peers, suppliers, and customers?
		3. Have you lined up your digital disruption ideas with your most impactful strategic choices using the Business Model Canvas or a similar framework?
		4. Have you looked at all three exponential possibilities—exponential technologies, exponential processes, and exponential ecosystems—to identify the most disruptive digital possibilities?
		5. Have you used a nonlinear ideation process, such as design thinking, to create new big ideas?
Partly Sync. (Stage 3)	**Effective Change Model**	1. Is there broad recognition and support, both among the leaders and the core organization, that change management will be ten times harder than the technology transformation itself?
		2. Have you sensed the conditions of the urgency to change vs. the organization's operating attitude toward change and made efforts to target a particular change situation?
		3. Have you deliberately chosen an appropriate strategy for change management, i.e., organic change, edge organization structure, or inorganic change?

Table A-1 Checklist of the surprising disciplines (*continued*)

Stage	Discipline	Questions
Partly Sync. (Stage 3) *Continued*	Effective Change Model	4. Have you identified the roles and people who will likely be the "frozen middle"?
		5. Have you designed new reward systems within the core to motivate the frozen middle into the change effort?
	Strategy Sufficiency	1. Have you designed mechanisms to generate a sufficient number of digital transformation projects in the core organization in an ongoing manner (intrapreneurship)?
		2. Do you have a mechanism that will allow you to take a select number of big, disruptive ideas from the pilot tests and scale them up rapidly?
		3. Do you have mechanisms, including risk/reward systems, that allow for at least 50 percent of your initiatives to fail forward?
		4. Have you separated resources and success criteria between the 70 (core operational activities), the 20 (continuous improvement activities of the core), and the 10 (disruptive innovation)?
		5. Have you identified the right metrics for success in order to celebrate digital transformation outcomes, not just corporate innovation theater activities?
Fully Synch. (Stage 4)	Digital Reorganization	1. Have you created a strategy and tangible plans to address people re-skilling for the digital era in terms of leadership and employee digital literacy, policies for human/machine interface, fluid organization structures, digital security, etc.?
		2. Has there been a strategy to combine the various digital/IT functions in the enterprise into an enabling digital resources function?

Table A-1 Checklist of the surprising disciplines (*continued*)

Stage	Discipline	Questions
Fully Synch. (Stage 4) *Continued*	Digital Reorganization	3. Has the digital resources function made plans to introduce more flexible and scalable technology platforms?
		4. Has the digital resources function upgraded its people capabilities to include more agility in execution, more expertise in new technology, and new capabilities to govern ecosystems?
		5. Have you updated your vendor ecosystem to line up with the skill sets necessary to win in the digitally transformed state?
	Staying Current	1. Have you created a strategy to help the organization stay current on digital technologies?
		2. Is there a focused top management digital literacy program that helps executives set the tone on the expectation of digital literacy?
		3. Are you fully leveraging VCs and start-ups to understand the latest disruptions in your industry?
		4. Have you enrolled your vendors, partners, and tech-savvy users to provide ongoing education for free?
		5. Have you fully explored creating open ecosystems to generate large numbers of innovative use cases internally and externally, e.g., by opening up your data via APIs to select developers?
Living DNA (Stage 5)	Agile Culture	1. Do you have an "agile culture" leg of your digital takeoff program that is aimed at sustaining ongoing transformation?
		2. Is there a strong, pervasive customer focus across the entire organization, and is your digital program going to further expand it?

Table A-1 Checklist of the surprising disciplines (*continued*)

Stage	Discipline	Questions
Living DNA (Stage 5) *Continued*	**Agile Culture**	3. Have you established a safe "fail forward" culture among the core/receiving organization that enables smart risk taking?
		4. Have you communicated and developed a common purpose across the organization that will support the perpetual transformation?
		5. Have you generated a spirit of constant evolution, i.e., your organization appreciates that "change is the only constant"?
	Sensing Risk	1. Have you incorporated a specific item in your annual strategy planning to sense and respond to digital disruption?
		2. Do you have a specific metric to gauge how much your industry is being digitally disrupted over time?
		3. Are you measuring quantitatively how much your customers are tilting the landscape toward digital disruption?
		4. Do you have a metric to capture how much the specific parts of your business model such as evolution of channels, partners, and activity systems are being transformed by digital?
		5. Are you measuring the state of investments in digital business and digital literacy in your enterprise?

Resource B

How to Use the Five Most Exponential Technologies

Though the list of exponential technologies is a moving target, there are five technologies that leaders cannot afford to lose track of. I call these the "Exponential Five." These are currently the most disruptive groups in general for enterprises. In this section, I provide a high-level primer on what they are and attempt to separate hype from reality.

The Exponential Five are:

1. Artificial intelligence

2. Smart process automation

3. Blockchain

4. Robotics and drones

5. Special-function technologies (virtual reality, 3D printing, Internet of Things, nanotech, energy storage, biotechnology, advanced materials, etc.)

1. Artificial Intelligence

If you had to pick only one exponential technology to focus on (and that would be a mistake!), it would most likely be artificial intelligence. AI is essentially the imitation of intelligent human behavior by computers or machines. It is the broadest way to think of computer intelligence. All other related terms are usually subsets of AI. So, machine learning is a subset of AI that ingests data to learn specific tasks. Deep learning, which became prominent when DeepMind's AlphaGo program beat the world Go champion, is in turn, a subset of machine learning. It is a way to solve complex problems using neural networks that simulate human decision making.

You are already a major consumer of AI technologies in your personal life. If you've used Siri, Cortana, or any other virtual assistant, you've already used AI. If you've had a credit card or bank proactively flag or block a transaction, you've experienced the fraud detection use of AI. If you've had Amazon, Netflix, or a similar service provider recommend a product based on your profile, that's AI too. Driverless cars use AI. An example that you might not know about—a huge number of simple stories that you read online on Yahoo!, AP, and others on financial summaries and sports results come from AI tools.

Understanding the Possibilities and Limitations of AI

AI may be all around us, but it is not omnipotent. The key to unlocking its vast potential lies in an innocuous but powerful term that's well known in IT circles—use cases. A "use case" is an application of a specific tool to a given problem. So, credit card fraud detection and machine-generated news articles are two use cases of AI. The reason why AI is suddenly so popular is that the number of use cases has hit a tipping point driven by affordable computing power. That phenomenon is true of all exponential technologies, but it's just that AI happens to be at the peak of the cycle.

The internet was one such exponential technology twenty years ago. It spawned an explosion of use cases. In fact, much of the dot-com boom was about innovators creating new use cases on top of the internet. Most of the early use cases on the internet were about "access" to stuff—buy products online, check your bank account, transact with your Bureau of Motor Vehicles. As the dot-com era died, it spun off a second generation of use cases that were in themselves further platforms to build even more use cases. Cloud computing is one such example. It essentially made computing server capacity available online to anyone with an internet connection, which in turn spun off a new generation of cloud-based software applications that were dramatically better than those that you had to physically install on your PC or your server. AI is experiencing a similar explosively growth of use cases.

Use Cases That Matter

The good news is that one doesn't need to be an expert in AI to understand the type of use cases that could help or disrupt your business model. Here are a few tips on AI that should help.

- You don't just "do" AI, like you don't "do" the internet. It's the use cases that matter.

- Therefore, beware of any vendor that's trying to sell you AI as a panacea or as a platform; you're in the use case race, not the AI race. Unless, of course, you're an AI developer.

- Most of the AI algorithms are open sourced. Any vendor selling you an AI platform is often packaging free stuff and probably selling it at a premium. There's some value in curated and packaged algorithms, but usually not as much as one would think.

- There are literally thousands of use cases possible in big enterprises. A small number of these will be critical to your future business model. Focus on those—follow the money.

- As a corollary, if your future business model depends on these few use cases, you probably want to develop some intellectual property in them to provide sustainable competitive advantage. Build enough AI and data science capabilities in-house for these.

Examples of Use Cases

AI can exist wherever human judgment is involved. In table B-1 below I have highlighted for illustration and inspiration only a few select categories of use cases broadly relevant to functions in most enterprises.

Table B-1 Illustrative use cases of AI in enterprises

Manufacturing	Business Processes	Marketing	Sales	Research and Development
Predictive maintenance	Automate shared service centers	Ad targeting	Accurate forecasting	Research literature and periodicals
Yield enhancement in manufacturing	Fraud management	Content generation	Sales rep. advising systems	Idea testing and validation
Efficient logistics	Personalized customer service	Customer segmentation	Intelligent routing	Neural networks for structural design
Optimize supply chain	Strong service reliability	Customer insights and offerings	Optimal shelving and merchandising	AI for imaging
Quality enhancement	Optimize talent	Best pricing	Trade funds ROI	Targeting candidates for testing

Practical Information You Need to Know

How do you identify use cases?

- Bring your best business experts and data scientists together to identify them. Even they will need to iterate and experiment frequently. Don't try to survey for use cases—experiment!

How do you build AI capabilities?

- Just do it. Hire a few data scientists. And most importantly, start gathering any and all types of data relevant to your business. AI is powerless without data.

Can AI be used in old-world industries?

- AI is still relevant there. With very few exceptions it's the combination of old + new that creates disruptive business models. Amazon's AI wouldn't be worth much without its logistics capabilities. You need to complement your old-world assets with new-world capabilities.

What are the effect of AI on jobs?

- As with any automation, AI will definitely repurpose people and skills. Your business plan needs to anticipate this.

Will AI destroy mankind?

- Probably not, because smart people are starting to raise the issue of boundaries for AI. But not investing in relevant AI capabilities for your business will sure as heck destroy your business!

2. Smart Process Automation

This is technology that uses software robots to further automate business processes in the enterprise that the base transactional systems could not. At one end of the smart process automation spectrum is robotic process automation (RPA), which includes software to automate any repetitive computer task. Think of it as superintelligent Excel macros that can work with any software on your computer. At the other end of the spectrum is AI, which helps with judgment-based transactions. Together, they have the ability to automate both structured as well as judgment-based tasks in the enterprise.

Software robots or smart process automation is emerging as a part of every organization's workforce. Software robots work 24/7/365.

They don't take breaks. And they can be simply copied to multiply your workforce. The downside—they work best with repetitive and structured tasks, although the addition of AI expands the capabilities to some judgment-based tasks.

There's an even more important reason to apply smart automation to work processes. The technology has reached a tipping point and delivers not just productivity gains but faster business cycles. It's the relatively quick and high rate of return of smart process automation that makes it disruptive. Depending on the complexity of the process, many smart process automation projects can be completed in a few weeks, pay out within a few months, and bring in the scalability (just copying the bots) and speed benefits as extras.

Examples of Smart Process Automation

Like AI, RPA can exist wherever humans do routine and repetitive knowledge tasks. Here's an illustrative list for inspiration. You will note that this list represents areas where basic automation (e.g., SAP, Salesforce, Oracle, Microsoft, and other large enterprise software) is already used. These "off the shelf" basic products cover only 50 to 90 percent of the automation needs in any enterprise, leaving gaps that coping mechanisms such as human touches, emails, and Excel sheets have to cover. This is a prime target for smart process automation.

- *Order processing, shipping, and billing*: Routine work, especially executed in offshore centers, involving multiple systems to complete the order management cycle.

- *Claims and underwriting processes*: Tasks especially in the insurance, banking, and manufacturing sectors involving significant human capacity in validating information routinely.

- *Customer or patient registration*: Activities that involve triggering downstream tasks in multiple systems. This whole process can be automated.

- *Credit card applications*: Although broadly applicable to processing structured requests, the credit card application process is an excellent illustration. It involves validating and authorizing eligibility across multiple sources of information.

- *Reporting and data management*: Tasks that involve pulling information from multiple sources and processing information in predictable ways.

- *Employee hiring and onboarding*: Automating activities that result from a new hire event, including updating multiple IT systems, organizing training, facilities, payroll, and so on.

- *Customer relations/complaints*: Structured processing of customer contacts across multiple departments in the organization.

- *Change of status processing (e.g., change of address)*: Routine tasks like changing parts of information for an entity.

Practical Information You Need to Know

Where should you start?

- Look for large numbers of employees doing routine tasks, whether done in-house or via your business process outsourcing (BPO) suppliers.

How big an idea is this?

- Pretty big. Many large implementations now target the use of one thousand or more robots, each of which could automate the tasks of several humans.

Can you add process reengineering and AI to RPA to multiply benefits?

- Don't automate a poorly designed process. Clean it up and then expand the automation to include judgmental tasks.

What type of organizations would benefit most?

- This helps traditional enterprises more than digitally native ones. Traditional enterprises tend to have large numbers of employees invested in routine knowledge-worker tasks. This is a good quick fix.

What are the cautions and limitations?

- First, you need to know what you're doing. In this case, internal business process and IT experts need to be heavily involved. Don't just outsource this task. Second, plan for ongoing operations. Who will change the bots when processes change?

3. Blockchain

Blockchain is the breakthrough underlying technology that was invented originally along with bitcoin. Whereas bitcoin is still highly speculative and not recommended for most enterprise use, blockchain is thought to be one of the most transformative technologies to have been invented since the internet. That's a big claim, but not without justification. It can disrupt activities related to managing transactions (e.g., bank transfers), just as the internet disrupted information access.

Think of blockchain as a digital ledger of transactions—a spreadsheet, if you will. Now imagine that this is duplicated thousands of times across many networks and constantly reconciled. What you get is an immutable record that's easily accessible but virtually impossible to corrupt because it constantly self-audits across the multiple copies. It is for this reason that blockchain is considered to be unhackable—at least for the moment.

The Possibilities of Blockchain

Because blockchain uses distributed data and is easy for multiple parties to access while still being highly secure, it's a tool that will disintermediate the middleman in any transaction. That's one of the reasons the financial industry is both nervous and excited about it. A large chunk of their work today is to intermediate between parties. In the securities trading arena, up to 10 percent of all transactions still have some error that needs to be manually addressed in order to settle trades. That is a multibillion-dollar saving opportunity in fees for cash settlement.

Another logical use would be in voting. While several countries are looking at the possibility of e-voting based on blockchain, several corporate and community organizations have already jumped on this. Abu Dhabi's stock exchange introduced e-voting for its annual general meetings. Estonia has use cases in validating services for residents and in corporate shareholder meetings.

Examples of Use Cases

The potential use cases are innumerable. Unsurprisingly, it turns out that the combination of highly decentralized transactions, easy access to many parties, and extremely high security can disrupt just about any transactional activity system. Just a few examples for illustration and inspiration appear in table B-2 below.

Table B-2 Illustrative use cases of blockchain

Financial Records and Models	Government Records	Supply Chain	Security	Emerging Markets
Cryptocurrencies	Land titles	Track and trace products and ingredients	Car/hotel/home/locker keys	Community microloans
Business transactions and records	Passports	Freight tracking and management	Secure vouchers/coupons/payments	Solar energy sharing
Trading	Birth/death certificates	Invoicing and payments	Betting records	Payments
Mortgage/loan records	e-voting	Contract management	Patents/copyright	Agriculture records
Microfinance	Government transparency	Supplier management	Digital rights management	Nonprofit records

Practical Information You Need to Know

Is blockchain overhyped?

- Yes, just like most disruptive technologies in their early stages. But that's not a good enough reason to ignore it. It's powerful enough to dramatically impact your business.

Regarding blockchain's unhackable claim—wasn't the bitcoin exchange Mt. Gox hacked?

- Yes. Although the blockchain itself was secure, the wallet keys to access the currency were not secured. It's like putting stuff in a vault but then being careless with the keys. It's a good lesson on the importance of strong, secure foundations for the infrastructure around the blockchain itself.

Where do you start with blockchain?

- Look at the intersection of transactions that need security and those that are distributed across parties. As with AI, start with reusing use cases that others have already created, which can be reapplied in quick and low-cost ways.

Where can you go to better understand blockchain's possibilities?

- There are plenty of resources online that list all the possible use cases of blockchain. Match that against your needs to get going. Think of developing new use cases when you've gained enough experience in the technology in your organization.

What are the cautions and limitations?

- There are a large number of limitations—but nothing that cannot be overcome. It's important to avoid overextending yourself with any emerging technology, including blockchain. Start small. Also, as with any exponential technology it's critical to understand what you're doing. Don't outsource it; in fact, never outsource something you don't understand.

4. Robotics and Drones

This section and the next one cover exponential capabilities that are either physical or special function in nature. If your business involves physical aspects, such as the creation, moving, retailing, or surveilling of items, then the capabilities in robotics or drones are tremendously rich in possibilities.

Robotics and drones have already crossed over from curiosity toys to serious disruptors. As of early 2017, drones have the power to lift more than five hundred pounds. And this keeps growing exponentially. Robots can already do last-mile product delivery, home assistance, warehouse operations, and security services. Some of the more innovative use cases, such as delivering blood supply to hospitals, are emerging from developing countries that have a need to leapfrog questionable local infrastructure. At this stage, enterprises aren't just testing capabilities but actively converting to drones and robotics.

Examples of Use Cases

Any task that needs physical seeing, sensing, assisting, moving, measuring, or delivering is fair game for robotics. Further, any of these tasks involving remote control is being targeted by drones. Naturally, new use cases emerge daily. A short list of industries that are already using robotics and drones is shown in table B-3 below.

Table B-3 Illustrative use cases of blockchain

Robotics	Drones
Manufacturing	Agriculture
Logistics and warehousing	Photography/Cinematography
Delivery	Journalism
Surgery and medicine	Remote monitoring of pipelines, wells, etc.
Home assistance	Forest and environment monitoring
Elderly care	Search and rescue
Retail merchandising	Military
Security	Package delivery
Military	Transportation
Construction	Warehouse management
Oil and gas	Bridges and other asset surveying
Disaster-related assistance	Real estate surveying
Police and civil services	Critical product delivery to remote areas
Hotels and restaurants	Security monitoring
Autonomous vehicles	Utilities maintenance
Entertainment	Insurance verification

Practical Information You Need to Know

What is the current stage of development for robotics and drones?

- It's more developed than most people think. Much further along than AI.

Which areas of businesses are likely to be affected?

- Look for your biggest cost, time, risk, or service-level opportunities involving physical movement.

How can you identify emerging use cases?

▪ Keep an eye out on start-up activity. Venture capitalist information sources as well as databases such as Crunchbase are an easy way to keep track of start-ups.

What about regulatory policies and approval processes?

▪ They're stabilizing incredibly fast. Drone operators used to need an airplane pilot's license. Now a simple drone pilot certification can be had by any sixteen-year-old with $150 and enough study material.

5. Special-Function Technologies

Whereas the above four exponential technologies are broadly applicable to most enterprises, there's a group of exponential technologies that are disruptive to specific industries. This includes fields like virtual reality, 3D printing, Internet of Things, nanotech, energy storage, biotechnology, and advanced materials. The complete list of special-function technologies is too big to cover in detail here, but the point to register is that these are likely to be disruptive in specific industries, e.g., 3D printing for equipment manufacturers or energy storage for traditional energy transmission enterprises. These deserve special attention in your digital transformation plans. Singularity University, the forward-looking think tank based in Silicon Valley, has arguably some of the best information on the implications of these special exponential technologies. Over the next few pages, I provide a brief glimpse of the amazing possibilities in two lesser-known areas.

The Disruptive Capabilities of Advanced Materials

What if your clothing could generate energy? A combination of fibers is being used to harvest energy from movement and from embedded fiber solar cells. Imagine if you could get cracks in your concrete structure to self-heal? Scientists are working on embedding bacteria in concrete that awaken when cracks appear and then produce limestone that fills the cracks. What if smart bricks in your home could "digest" pollutants and generate energy at the same time? These innovative bricks include microbial fuel cells with programmable synthetic microorganisms. When activated, they can clean water, reclaim phosphate, or generate electricity. These are a few examples of new materials that are rapidly changing the landscape of traditional materials science.

Collectively, the term "advanced materials" describes substances that demonstrate major improvements over traditional materials that have been in use for several years. What's unique about advanced materials is the availability of cheap computing capacity to dramatically accelerate the pace at which new breakthroughs can be created. This effect is similar to the disruptive impact of genomics in medicine and can no longer be ignored.

The Possibilities of a Smarter World

The other exponential technology that deserves more attention is smart devices. We have been traditionally trained to think of the world as having two types of objects—smart and dumb. So, our self-driving car can be smart, but the roadway is dumb. What if this assumption could be turned on its head? What if the road was as smart as the car? This gets us into the amazing possibilities of the internet of everything (Internet of Things).

The Internet of Things, or IoT, is interconnecting the physical and digital worlds in unprecedented ways. Essentially, IoT is an interconnected network of devices that can collect or exchange data. It can do this remotely, thereby opening up possibilities that range from smart toasters to smart parking spaces, smart health monitors, real-time energy optimization, and smart manufacturing.

How Can We Make Everything Smart?

Think of a single IoT device as a special-purpose sensor that measures and transmits necessary information and can be made smart enough to make some decisions. A Nest thermostat does this with temperature, carbon monoxide, and video image information. By using this data, it can help cut energy consumption in your home dramatically.

Now imagine if a large number of such smart IoT devices—your toothbrush, TV, home security system, lawn mower, car, cleaning robot, toaster, coffee maker, fridge, washer and dryer, computer, bed, showerhead, along with your digital information, such as your online shopping account, your credit card data, your music collection, your contacts, and your personal preferences—were able to seamlessly and intelligently work with each other. So, while you were away at work, your refrigerator would order groceries that were running low, the lawn mower and floor-cleaning robot would run their cycles, your security system would intelligently allow the right deliveries, and your washing machine would sense that it's running low on laundry detergent and place an order. As you arrive home, the home security system would recognize you and open the door, the music system would start playing your favorites, the oven would start reheating your meal, the trash can would message you that it's full, and your smartphone would help you order an Uber to the airport at exactly the right moment, based on real-time traffic information.

Now think of what would be possible if a large number of smart homes were networked together with other sensors to make smart cities. Problems of security, environment, congestion, public services, medical treatment, and financial services could be addressed more efficiently.

Finally, think of the possibilities as applied to the enterprise. Smart factories could virtually run themselves. Smart transportation could optimize service and costs. Smart retailing could personalize services to your customers.

It is this ability to bring together the physical world and the digital world, and to do this across a large-scale network, that will disrupt our lives as part of the Fourth Industrial Revolution.

Every Industry Has One or More Special-Function Disruptive Technologies

Although we've touched upon only a few special-function disruptive technologies, the point is that these industry-specific capabilities possess the most direct power to upend your business model. Manufacturing will be directly disrupted by 3D printing, advanced materials, IoT, nanotech, and many more emerging technologies. The ability to recognize and leverage the right combination of special-function disruptive technologies for the digital era for your business model is your best bet to avoid being disrupted.

Practical Information You Need to Know

Where do you start with special-function technologies?

- Start by constantly reviewing your business strategy and customer needs so it incorporates the right special-function disruptive technologies. Innovate for new products and services and with new disruptive business models. Bring in sufficient organizational capability to help you assess possibilities and risks.

Are all these new technologies affordable?

- This doesn't need to be expensive. You may be able to iterate in small, low-cost cycles initially, or partner with others. And not all technologies need additional new investment. Let's take IoT sensors—if the driver of your logistics truck has a smartphone, then you have an IoT sensor already. Most manufacturing facilities have sensors in machines that are heavily underutilized.

What is the maturity of special-function tech capabilities?

- It's important to think of the maturity of special-function exponential technologies differently, since these are on the leading edge of disruption for your industry. It may be necessary to err on the side of investing in some industry-disruptive applications rather than waiting for the world to pass you by.

Notes

1. Caletha Crawford, "Cushman & Wakefield's Retail Predictions for 2018 Are Not What You Want to Hear," Sourcing Journal, January 10, 2018, https://sourcingjournal.com/topics/business-news /retail-apocalypse-2018-cushman-wakefield-prediction-76866 [accessed December 19, 2018].

2. CB Insights Research, "Here Are 40 Casualties of the Retail Apocalypse and Why They Failed," October 17, 2018, https://www .cbinsights.com/research/retail-apocalypse-timeline-infographic [accessed December 19, 2018].

3. Rebecca McClay, "2018: The Year of Retail Bankruptcies," Investo- pedia, August 3, 2018, https://www.investopedia.com/news/year -retail-bankruptcies-looms-m/ [accessed December 19, 2018].

4. Michael Bucy et al., "The 'How' of Transformation," McKinsey & Company, May 2016, https://www.mckinsey.com/industries/retail /our-insights/the-how-of-transformation [accessed December 19, 2018].

5. Nadir Hirji and Gale Geddes, "What's Your Digital ROI? Realizing the Value of Digital Investments," Strategy&/PwC, October 12, 2016, https://www.strategyand.pwc.com/report/whats-your -digital-ROI [accessed December 19, 2018].

6. Michael Sheetz, "Technology Killing Off Corporate America: Average Life Span of Companies Under 20 Years," CNBC, August 24, 2017, https://www.cnbc.com/2017/08/24/technology -killing-off-corporations-average-lifespan-of-company-under-20 -years.html [accessed December 19, 2018].

7. Bruce Rogers, "Why 84% of Companies Fail at Digital Transforma- tion," Forbes.com, January 7, 2016, https://www.forbes.com/sites /brucerogers/2016/01/07/why-84-of-companies-fail-at-digital -transformation/#14f3cddc397b [accessed December 19, 2018].

8. Art & Architecture Quarterly, "Long Island Museum: The Carriage Collection," http://www.aaqeastend.com/contents/portfolio/long -island-museum-carriage-collection-finest-collection-of-horse -drawn-vehicles/ [accessed December 19, 2018].

9. Park City Museum, "Transportation in America and the Carriage Age," September 2007, https://parkcityhistory.org/wp-content /uploads/2012/04/Teacher-Background-Information.pdf [accessed December 19, 2018].

10. Kent C. Boese, "From Horses to Horsepower: Studebaker Helped Move a Nation," Smithsonian Libraries, http://www.sil.si.edu /ondisplay/studebaker/intro.htm [accessed December 19, 2018].

11. Richard M. Langworth, *Studebaker 1946–1966: The Classic Post-war Years* (Minneapolis, MN: Motorbooks International, 1993).

12. Boese, "From Horses to Horsepower."

13. B.R., "A Crash Course in Probability," *The Economist*, January 29, 2015, https://www.economist.com/gulliver/2015/01/29/a-crash -course-in-probability [accessed December 19, 2018].

14. Salim Ismail, Michael S. Malone, and Yuri van Geest. *Exponential Organizations: Why New Organizations Are Ten Times Better, Faster, and Cheaper Than Yours—And What to Do About It* (New York: Diversion Books, 2014).

15. BT Group, "Digital Transformation Top Priority for CEOs, Says New BT and EIU Research," GlobalServices.bt.com, September 12, 2017, https://www.globalservices.bt.com/en/aboutus/news-press /digital-transformation-top-priority-for-ceos [accessed December 19, 2018].

16. Gartner, "Gartner 2016 CEO and Senior Business Executive Survey Shows That Half of CEOs Expect Their Industries to Be Substantially or Unrecognizably Transformed by Digital," https://www .gartner.com/newsroom/id/3287617 [accessed December 19, 2018].

17. Josh Bersin, "Digital Leadership Is Not an Optional Part of Being a CEO," *Harvard Business Review*, December 1, 2016, https://hbr. org/2016/12/digital-leadership-is-not-an-optional-part-of-being -a-ceo [accessed December 19, 2018].

18. Ibid.

19. Calleam Consulting, "Denver Airport Baggage System Case Study," 2008, http://calleam.com/WTPF/?page_id=2086 [accessed December 19, 2018].

20. Kirk Johnson, "Denver Airport Saw the Future. It Didn't Work," *New York Times*, August 27, 2005, https://www.nytimes.com /2005 /08/27/us/denver-airport-saw-the-future-it-didnt-work.html [accessed December 19, 2018].

21. Justin Bariso, "What Your Business Can Learn From Netflix," Inc.com, December 4, 2015, https://www.inc.com/justin-bariso /the-secrets-behind-the-extraordinary-success-of-netflix.html [accessed December 19, 2018].

22. Timothy Stenovec, "One Reason for Netflix's Success—It Treats Employees Like Grownups," Huffington Post, December 6, 2017, https://www.huffingtonpost.com/2015/02/27/netflix-culture-deck -success_n_6763716.html [accessed December 19, 2018].

23. Chris Ueland, "A 360 Degree View of the Entire Netflix Stack," *High Scalability* (blog), November 9, 2015, http://highscalability .com/blog/2015/11/9/a-360-degree-view-of-the-entire-netflix -stack.html [accessed December 19, 2018].

24. Larry Barrett and Sean Gallagher, "Fast Food Fails Digital Network-ing Test," *Baseline*, http://www.baselinemag.com/c/a/Projects -Supply-Chain/McDonalds-McBusted [accessed February 7, 2019].

25. Larry Barrett and Sean Gallagher, "Fast Food Fails Digital Net-working Test," *Baseline*, July 2, 2003, http://www.base linemag.com /c/a/Projects-Supply-Chain/McDonalds-McBusted [accessed December 19, 2018].

26. Spencer E. Ante, "Case Study: Bank of America," June 18, 2006, Bloomberg, https://www.bloomberg.com/news/articles/2006-06 -18/case-study-bank-of-america [accessed December 19, 2018].

27. John Hagel III, John Seely Brown, and Lang Davison, "How to Bring the Core to the Edge," *Harvard Business Review*, February 6, 2009, https://hbr.org/2009/02/how-to-bring-the-edge-to-the-c.html [accessed December 19, 2018].

28. Ismail et al., *Exponential Organizations*.

29. Jonathan L. S. Byrnes, "Middle Management Excellence," jlbyrnes .com, December 5, 2005, http://jlbyrnes.com/uploads/Main /Middle Management Excellence HBSWK 12-05.pdf [accessed December 19, 2018].

30. Quentin Hardy, "Google's Innovation—and Everyone's?" Forbes.com, July 16, 2011, https://www.forbes.com/sites /quentinhardy /2011/07/16/googles-innovation-and-everyones /#4a314d4a3066 [accessed December 19, 2018].

31. Bansi Nagji and Geoff Tuff, "Managing Your Innovation Portfolio," *Harvard Business Review*, May 2012, https://hbr.org/2012/05 /managing-your-innovation-portfolio [accessed December 19, 2018].

32. Biography, "Richard Branson," https://www.biography.com
    /people/richard-branson-9224520 [accessed December 19, 2018].

33. Richard Feloni, "Why Richard Branson Is So Successful," Business
    Insider, February 11, 2015, https://www.businessinsider.com/how
    -richard-branson-maintains-the-virgin-group-2015-2 [accessed
    December 19, 2018].

34. Richard Branson, "Richard Branson on Intrapreneurs," msnbc.com,
    January 31, 2011, http://www.nbcnews.com/id/41359235/ns
    /business-small_business/t/richard-branson-intrapreneurs
    /#.XBqusWhKg2w [accessed December 19, 2018].

35. Gianna Scorsone, "5 Hot and High-Paying Tech Skills for 2018,"
    CIO.com, April 23, 2018, https://www.cio.com/article/3269251/it
    -skills-training/5-hot-and-high-paying-tech-skills-for-2018.html
    [accessed December 19, 2018].

36. Susan Caminiti, "4 Gig Economy Trends That Are Radically
    Transforming the US Job Market," CNBC, October 29, 2018,
    https://www.cnbc.com/2018/10/29/4-gig-economy-trends-that
    -are-radically-transforming-the-us-job-market.html [accessed
    December 19, 2018].

37. Susan Caminiti, "AT&T's $1 Billion Gambit: Retraining Nearly Half
    Its Workforce for Jobs of the Future," CNBC, March 13, 2018,
    https://www.cnbc.com/2018/03/13/atts-1-billion-gambit-retraining
    -nearly-half-its-workforce.html [accessed December 19, 2018].

38. John Donovan and Cathy Benko, "AT&T's Talent Overhaul,"
    Harvard Business Review, October 2016, https://hbr.org/2016/10
    /atts-talent-overhaul [accessed December 19, 2018].

39. Prachi Bhardwaj, "An Adobe Executive Once Accidentally Leaked
    Plans to the Press Before Discussing Them with the CEO—And It
    Was the Best Thing to Happen to the Company's Productivity,"
    Business Insider, July 14, 2018, https://www.businessinsider.com
    /adobe-donna-morris-productivity-hr-2018-7 [accessed
    December 19, 2018].

40. David Burkus, "How Adobe Scrapped Its Performance Review
    System and Why It Worked," Forbes.com, June 1, 2016,
    https://www.forbes.com/sites/davidburkus/2016/06/01/how
    -adobe-scrapped-its-performance-review-system-and-why-it
    -worked/#64fd21fa55e8 [accessed December 19, 2018].

41. David Burkus, "Inside Adobe's Innovation Kit," Harvard Business
    Review, February 23, 2015, https://hbr.org/2015/02/inside-adobes
    -innovation-kit [accessed December 19, 2018].

42. Infinit Contact, "10 Zappos Stories That Will Change the Way You Look at Customer Service Forever," infinitcontact.com, October 29, 2013, https://www.infinitcontact.com/blog/zappos-stories-that -will-change-the-way-you-look-at-customer-service [accessed December 19, 2018].

43. Tony Hsieh, "How I Did It: Tony Hsieh, CEO, Zappos.com," Inc. com, September 1, 2006, https://www.inc.com/magazine/20060901 /hidi-hsieh.html [accessed December 20, 2018].

44. Craig Silverman, "How to Create a Culture and Structure for Innovation," American Press Institute, May 27, 2015, https://www .americanpressinstitute.org/publications/reports/strategy-studies /culture-and-structure-for-innovation/ [accessed December 19, 2018].

45. Joshua Benton, "The Leaked New York Times Innovation Report Is One of the Key Documents of This Media Age," Nieman Lab, May 15, 2014, http://www.niemanlab.org/2014/05/the-leaked-new-york -times-innovation-report-is-one-of-the-key-documents -of-this-media-age/ [accessed December 19, 2018].

46. Allana Akhtar, "Elon Musk Says SpaceX Didn't Have a Business Model When It Started," Money.com, March 12, 2018, http://time .com/money/5195687/elon-musk-business-model-space-x [accessed December 19, 2018].

47. Marco della Cava, "Elon Musk: Rockets and Electric Cars 'Dumbest' Possible Business Ventures," *USA Today*, March 12, 2018, https://www.usatoday.com/story/tech/2018/03/12/elon-musk-sxsw -rockets-and-electric-cars-dumbest-possible-business-ventures /416670002/ [accessed December 19, 2018].

48. Louis Anslow, "SpaceX: A History of Fiery Failures," Timeline.com, September 1, 2016, https://timeline.com/spacex-musk-rocket -failures-c22975218fbe [accessed December 19, 2018].

49. IBM, "The C-Suite Study," https://www.ibm.com/services/insights /c-suite-study [accessed December 19, 2018].

50. Chunka Mui, "How Kodak Failed," Forbes.com, January 18, 2012, https://www.forbes.com/sites/chunkamui/2012/01/18/how-kodak -failed/#67b8a2fa6f27 [accessed December 19, 2018].

51. Maxwell Wessel, "Why Preventing Disruption in 2017 Is Harder Than It Was When Christensen Coined the Term," *Harvard Business Review*, September 4, 2017, https://hbr.org/2017/09/why -preventing-disruption-in-2017-is-harder-than-it-was-when -christensen-coined-the-term [accessed December 19, 2018]

Acknowledgments

I may have written the words, but Steve Piersanti, my editor, turned them into a book. Steve also happens to be the founder and president of Berrett-Koehler, which has to be the most author-supportive publisher in the world. Steve didn't just edit; he also helped me conceptualize the idea, challenged and inspired me, and stretched my thinking endlessly. This book has hugely benefited from Steve's touches. Steve—I owe you. Big time!

The staff at BK were equally impressive. Jeevan Sivasubramaniam ran a tight ship to keep things moving like clockwork. Michael Crowley led the superb team from sales and marketing who ran an enviable world-class operation. I should know—I used to work for a great marketing company! My sincere thanks to Lasell Whipple, Design Director, for her patient and brilliant design, including the striking cover; Edward Wade, Director of Design and Production, for production support; David Marshall for editorial and digital support; María Jesús Aguiló and Catherine Lengronne for outstanding work on the licensing of local versions; Leslie Crandell for making my life so easy on US sales and support; Liz McKellar for stellar work on international rights; and Courtney Schonfeld for a brilliant audio version. Jon Ford, the super capable copy editor, and Jon Peck the brilliant page editor from Dovetail Publishing Services, made the editing process a breeze. Cathy Lewis, from CS Lewis Publicity was masterful in PR planning and execution. The one and only Jill Totenberg proved why she is known in the business as one of the best tier one PR agents around. These are but a fraction of the amazing people who are Berrett-Koehler employees and partners.

The Procter & Gamble family has been a nurturing support structure and an endless source of learning and friendships for half my living years (and truth be told, within those years, more than half the twenty-four hours in a day). But it's always been fun! Bob McDonald was an inspiring and uplifting leader from the early days in the Philippines. Thanks, Bob, also for the wonderful foreword. I was extremely fortunate with my last

205

two bosses at P&G, Filippo Passerini and Julio Nemeth. They were both brilliant, visionary, immaculately skilled, and intensely warm hearted.

The Next Generation Services team at P&G were always much more than colleagues; they were extended family. Brent Duersch was a partner in crime from day one. Kim Eldridge, my assistant, was a consummate professional, cheerleader and group mother all rolled into one. Vasanthi Chalasani, who succeeded me, continues to take the team to greater heights. The scale-partner companies—Ascendum, EY, Genpact, Infosys, L&T Infotech, HCL, HPE/DXC, Tata Consultancy Services, Wipro, and WNS—brought more than expertise; they were a source of passion and intense collaboration.

Salim Ismail has been an advisor and father figure throughout this journey. Granted, an extremely young father figure, but one nonetheless. The OpenExO team has been a fantastic resource along the way— Samantha McMahon, Michelle Lapierre, Francisco Palao Reinés, and Emilie Sydney-Smith—a big thank you! Michael Leadbetter, president and founder of Pivot Factory, has been a partner, friend, supporter in chief, and fellow foodie. Thanks, Michael!

Several individuals were a tremendous help during the early days when I had little idea on how to write or publish a book. Don Fehr, my agent from the legendary Trident Media Group, took a chance on an unknown author and coached me into something resembling respectability. To Bob Johansen, Distinguished Fellow at the Institute for the Future, thanks for guidance and the recommendation to Berrett-Koehler. My dear friend Venkat Srinivasan, author and serial founder, provided helpful advice and made great connections. Dr. Sanjiv Chopra, prolific author and faculty member at Harvard Medical School, opened doors to the publishing world. Authors Simone Ahuja from Blood Orange, Paul Butler from GlobalEdg, Dan Roberts from Ouellette & Associates, and Jose Ignacio Sordo from CIO Eureka patiently showed me the ropes on being a writer.

Dr. Vinisha Peres was a dream researcher. Joe Lowenstein, veteran pilot and a genuine nice guy, happily provided aviation expertise that would have taken me several decades of personal flying experience to acquire. Sharad Malhautra was a constant resource throughout the journey. Rajan and Alka Panandiker, ace photography hobbyists (and, I must mention, fellow Goans), have my gratitude for their huge investment of time.

I am a big believer in the power of ecosystems, and this book was a perfect vehicle for me to tap into a vast pool of specialists. BK's expert-network members Travis Wilson, Mike McNair, David Marshall, Nic Albert, Amity Bacon, and Douglas Hammer provided detailed reviews that helped shape this book tremendously.

A few close and respected colleagues invested significant effort to provide detailed manuscript critique, which helped me reshape the book significantly toward the end: Mike Lingle, a.k.a. the Editing Wiz, Mark Dorfmueller, Guniz Louit, Sanjay Jiandani, Suman Sasmal, German Faraoni, Nicolas Kerling, Brent Duersch, Brad Comerford, Anshul Srivastava, Brad Humphries, Gaurav Mathur, Parthiv Sheth, and Udayan Dasgupta. Thank you so much for your passion.

Paola Lucetti, Carlos Amesquita, Sanjay Singh, Yazdi Bagli, Kshitij Mulay, Kishore Karuppan, Mattijs Kersten, Clyde Bailey, Alfredo Colas, Kelsey Driscoll, Gautam Chander, Mike Teo, and Oana Laza—thanks for your support.

The ExO Consultant ecosystem was another key expert network that provided incredibly helpful insights based on their practical experience. In particular Ann Ralston, Michal Monit, Rodrigo Castro Cordero, and Almira Radjab played a significant role in bringing real-life experience into the work.

Book endorsers play a vital role in providing their professional input and support to the effort. A simple thank-you is insufficient. To my endorsers—you helped me tremendously via your own credibility.

I've used the word "family" a few times above to describe the ultimate in relationships, because that's how I truly feel about what my biological one has given me. My parents, Ernest and Veronica Saldanha, personified selfless giving and endless love. My siblings and their spouses Marilyn and Ambrose, Ivy and Charlie, and Flory and Cliffy have shown that the sky is the limit when a call for help comes in. My mother-in-law, Ermelinda Fernandes, who passed away recently, never stopped thinking of ways in which she could spread education.

My daughters, Lara and Rene, have been a bigger inspiration, source of help, and grounding than they will ever realize. They worked on the manuscript along with me and brought a certain millennial flavor to the whole effort with their comments ("I don't think I can help because your manuscript has too many problems") and suggestions

("Use the picture of you being attacked by the parrot for your cover if you want your book to sell").

Finally, a very special thanks to my wife and pillar of support, Julia. Her love, inspiration, and collaboration on every stage of this book have been tremendous. This book wouldn't have been possible without her.

Index

Page numbers followed by *f* or *t* indicate a figure or table.

About the Author

For over three decades, Tony Saldanha has been a globally recognized business and technology leader on the forefront of the global business services and information technology industry. This book is the culmination of personal experiences in hands-on operation, disruptive innovation, and strategy over this time.

Tony's experience in digital transformation runs deep. During a twenty-seven-year career at Procter & Gamble, he ran both operations and digital transformation for P&G's famed GBS and IT organization in every region of the world, ending up as Global Shared Services and Information Technology Vice President. As a well-known industry thought leader, he has led GBS design and operations, held CIO positions, managed acquisitions and divestitures, ran large-scale outsourcing, created industry-wide disruptive innovation structures, and designed new business models. He was named on *Computerworld*'s Premier 100 IT Professionals list in 2013.

Tony has had a ringside view of the transformative power of digital technology all his life. Growing up in India in the '70s and '80s, he personally experienced the dramatic change that software technology brought to individuals, organizations, and societies. That first-hand experience of the digital revolution continued through his work in sixty-plus countries and by having lived in six countries. Tony created business efficiency via standardization in the 1990s when he gave out PCs with free order-processing software to all P&G distributors in Asia. PCs were not cheap then, but the standardization that P&G got in return was worth much more in operational efficiencies. He helped the development of the outsourcing industry when he program-managed the biggest global IT outsourcing deal in the world, worth $8 billion in 2003 for P&G. Tony led the absorption of the $10 billion Gillette company's operations into P&G systems as Gillette

CIO in 2005. In 2009, he moved on to creating new digital business models while leading P&G IT and shared services for Central and Eastern Europe, the Middle East, and Africa. The new technology-enabled capabilities for selling and distribution ended up providing better performance in places such as Nigeria than in the entire developed world.

The recent opportunity to redo digital capabilities for Global Business Services at P&G, by using exponential digital capabilities from the Fourth Industrial Revolution, has brought together all of Tony's digital transformation experiences against the big challenge of industry-level disruption. In tackling this monstrous challenge, it became apparent that this transformation would be successful only if he could beat the 70 percent failure odds of digital transformation projects. Driven by this insight, Tony's focus over the recent years has not been on technology but on the anthropological and engineering rigor that is necessary to deliver successful digital transformations.

Tony is currently an advisor to boards and C-suite executives on digital transformation. He continues to be a sought-after speaker in his spare time. Tony also advises several start-ups and venture capitalists. He has founded a blockchain-based company to help the IT industry commercialize disruptive software. Tony's prior board experience includes IT advisory board memberships at the University of Cincinnati, the Indiana University business intelligence program, and the University of Texas. He has been on the customer advisory boards of Cloudera, Box, and High Radius. Among nonprofits, Tony was the founding member and chairman of the board for the INTERalliance of Greater Cincinnati and is currently on the boards of Community Shares of Greater Cincinnati and Remineralize the Earth.

Tony and his wife, Julia, have two daughters. They reside in Cincinnati, Ohio.

Dear reader,

Thank you for picking up this book and welcome to the worldwide BK community! You're joining a special group of people who have come together to create positive change in their lives, organizations, and communities.

What's BK all about?

Our mission is to connect people and ideas to create a world that works for all.

Why? Our communities, organizations, and lives get bogged down by old paradigms of self-interest, exclusion, hierarchy, and privilege. But we believe that can change. That's why we seek the leading experts on these challenges—and share their actionable ideas with you.

A welcome gift

To help you get started, we'd like to offer you a **free copy** of one of our bestselling ebooks:

www.bkconnection.com/welcome

When you claim your **free ebook**, you'll also be subscribed to our blog.

Our freshest insights

Access the best new tools and ideas for leaders at all levels on our blog at ideas.bkconnection.com.

Sincerely,

Your friends at Berrett-Koehler